trotman

WINNING
interviews for
first-time
job hunters

WINNING
interviews for first-time job hunters

KATHLEEN HOUSTON

Winning Interviews for First-time Job Hunters
This first edition published in 2004 by Trotman and Company Ltd
2 The Green, Richmond, Surrey TW9 1PL

Reprinted 2004
Reprinted 2006

© Trotman and Company Limited 2004

Editorial and Publishing Team
Author Kathleen Houston
Editorial Mina Patria, Editorial Director; Rachel Lockhart, Commissioning Editor; Anya Wilson, Editor; Bianca Knights, Assistant Editor
Production Ken Ruskin, Head of Pre-press and Production
Sales and Marketing Suzanne Johnson Marketing Manager
Advertising Tom Lee, Commercial Director

Design by XAB

British Library Cataloguing in Publication Data
A catalogue record for this book is available from the British Library

ISBN 0 85660 972 2

Typeset by Mac Style Ltd, Scarborough, N. Yorkshire
Printed and bound in Great Britain by Bell & Bain Ltd, Glasgow, Scotland

contents

We have ways of
making you talk –
First thoughts
about interviews

Here's your mission, if you are prepared to accept it – you're going to find out everything there is to know about interviews. In the early stages, you'll confirm what you probably already knew, which is that you, like most people, find interviews somewhat stressful. But here's my promise to you – at a point part way through your mission, you'll suddenly find that you know so much about interviews, and what really goes on, that the fear factor will begin to recede and be replaced by a sense of comforting familiarity about the whole interview game.

That won't be the end though – turning fear into familiarity is just the start. Next I predict that you will begin to develop an expertise on interview performance and know just what this is about. This will mean that you won't be complacent about interviews but will be sure about what you have to do to make the most out of the interview situation, presenting yourself as the perfect applicant – an amazing and resourceful person who will be irresistible to any potential interviewer.

These may sound like grand claims, but don't tell me you're not the tiniest bit curious about just how this transformation process can take place. You are? Then you will need to accept the mission in full, which will require you to be courageous and bold and learn everything you need to know, taking the time to evaluate your own unique capabilities and selling points so that you can present yourself at interview as an authentic and compelling applicant.

On being authentic

Employers who interview applicants frequently complain about interviewees who seem fake – they claim that some interviewees come across as the worst kind of snake-oil salesman, while others don't seem to project just who they are in a real way.

Many applicants, it seems, try too hard and seem false; others freeze and come across as Mr, Mrs or Ms Blank. It may be that you're thinking that it's a no-win situation – either you project yourself in a **performing** kind of way (and so they think you are acting and are therefore a fake) or you go in and **be yourself** and that might be scared/anxious/numb/modest/unassuming due to the rather false circumstances of an interview (and so they think you are withdrawn and uncommunicative).

Well, here's the secret formula that it is your mission to find and guard – **you can perform and be yourself** in the somewhat false and contrived situation of the interview – and that's what people who have winning interview skills do. Being authentic is simply about the following obvious and basic imperatives –

SHOW UP   – that means, turn up for the interview on time, in the right place
SHOW UP   – that means, put yourself on show, dress up, make sure you look good
SHOW UP   – that means, be prepared to show what you can do by telling them how you fit their requirements
SHOW OFF – this is the hard one that puts many people off, but stay with me on this. This is not about saying, 'I am the greatest,' but it is about saying something along the lines of 'Your advert asked for a tightrope walker and I can do that really well!'

By 'showing' who you are, you are being truly authentic and sending out the signal 'I really want this job and believe I can do it well.' There's nothing fake about that! The weird thing is that when people act modestly, generally it isn't honest at all, and interviewers could be forgiven for thinking something like – 'This person who says he can tightrope walk quite well is not being big-headed, but can I be sure he/she can do the job every circus night without falling?'

interviewtip

Perform and be yourself!

So, acting modestly or acting arrogantly is not what being authentic is about; allowing the 'real you' to shine out is. Unfortunately, that 'real you' can be obscured or hidden by nerves, and sometimes that nervousness is misread by interviewers as lack of ability for – or even lack of interest in – the job.

This is due to the fact that non-verbal or body-language signals, though powerful, are read or judged with less precision than verbal language. So someone can clearly say

'I would love to be offered this job!'

but this will probably be convincing **only** if the person's tone and body language match her words.

If someone has a face that seems to be tense and his eye contact isn't steady (both frequent symptoms of nervousness), the interviewer might wrongly assume that this is due to lack of interest. What I mean to help you realise is how you can 'project' in an authentic way, taking control of your own performance at interview so that all your signals are clear and direct.

If you're still wondering how words like 'performance' and 'project' can be part of being 'real' and 'authentic', you need to read on – it will, I promise, become entirely clear.

Ways to make you talk

Finally, on the subject of 'ways to make you talk', I need to banish images of interrogation and torture from your mind, while impressing on you that **interviews are about you talking most of the time.** Without that, interviewers can't really know enough about you to make what might, for them, be a costly recruitment decision.

You wouldn't buy a CD or DVD without listening to or viewing it – the cover or recommendations might not be enough to convince you. You have to see how it plays. In the same way, your wonderful CV (see my *Winning CVs for First-time Job Hunters*, published by Trotman) and application, even your references, may have made them interested, but they want to see you strut your stuff, so it's their job to 'make you talk' and your job to be responsive.

The format of this book is planned to take you through from interview fears to how to give an authentic and winning performance at an interview. It will work best if you follow it logically – from cover to cover – but decide what works best for you. I can't guarantee that you'll get the job every time (or I would seem like that snake-oil salesman myself), but I can assure you that you will be able to 'turn on' a good interview performance that will make you feel like a winner, regardless of whether your interviewers have had the sense to recruit you.

Recruitment decisions are complex and are often decided on more than a brilliant interview performance, but the general rule is that a good interview is the clincher – the factor that convinces the employer to take the plunge. Nonetheless, 99 per cent of people I coach for interviews have been offered the jobs they were interviewed for. So I know this stuff works and can therefore commend it to you wholeheartedly.

Rational and irrational interview fears – What these are and how to conquer them

It's a normal day and you meet someone at a bus stop and a conversation develops. Bus-stop person asks you casually about yourself and what you do. You tell them about your recent studies or a previous or current job, and they show interest and ask you more questions. You chat away, and they gain an impression of you and what you are like and what motivates you.

What is amazing about this scenario is that almost everyone in this situation is relaxed and fairly 'real'. Let me ask you this – in this kind of situation, is it likely that you would

1 have sweaty palms?

2 experience stomach churning?

3 find your mind going blank?

4 wonder what to say next, how long to talk or when to stop?

5 not know what to say?

Of course, the above are all common reactions to interview situations but rarely occur in casual conversations.

The reality is that we have conversations like this every day when we reveal ourselves to people by acting naturally. A student I met at a local college described to me just such an event, which was in fact a conversation in a fish-and-chip shop queue. This is how it went –

Random Person	Hey, this is going to take some time by the look of the queue.
Student	Yeah, it looks pretty busy and I'm starving. The college restaurant was closed when I got there.
Random Person	Which college do you go to?
Student	I go to Barmy College.
Random Person	I've heard that's a good college – what do you do there?
Student	I'm doing a media studies course which covers web design, and that's the project I've been working on

	today. I love doing interesting things on the web and coming up with my own ideas. Today it went really well, and my tutor was pretty impressed because I had interpreted the design brief in a surprising way.
Random Person	There's still ten people in front of us! So tell me what you did.
Student	Well, we had to come up with a website for a dog-food firm, and I downloaded some gorgeous pictures of cute dogs to liven up their dull website, changed the colours, the typography and freshened up the copy on the site.
Random Person	That sounds great! I'm wondering whether you'd take a look at my website. I run a small garden-furniture firm, and it's hard to make that seem interesting. I'd pay you for some advice and consultancy. Would you be interested? Here's my card. Give me a ring ... Oh cod and chips twice, please!

Now, that might seem a little strange to you, but we have conversations like these with random people every day. There are three important things to realise about these conversations:

1 They are not conversations, but interviews in disguise!

2 Consider them interview practice and take the opportunity to talk to strange people who want to know about you in this extremely natural way.

3 They are in fact a major component in a skill called networking, which is the primary way you can seek out job opportunities and even actual job offers.

Interviews are just conversations in disguise

There is a protocol to conversations, which only occasionally gets disrupted by over-talkative people. Generally they work, as you know, on a reciprocal basis – you say something, someone says something back. Sometimes one person talks more, probably because the questioner is very interested in what the responder is saying. Typically you do not worry about the words you use or how you phrase them because you are at ease and it comes naturally.

You may be thinking that random conversations do not have the same burden of expectation as interviews, but it is really useful to reframe your idea of an interview as a structured conversation with a purpose.

In fact, if you could think to yourself

'I'm just going to have a conversation with them about a job that I think would suit me',

it could prompt you into a more resourceful frame of mind than if you thought –

'They're going to interview me for a job.'

On the frame-of-mind spectrum, interviews are rated something like this –

Interrogation	Interview	Conversation
Torture	Them against me	Questions back and forth
Intrusive questions	Being examined	Discovery
Fast pace	Nerve-wracking	Interest
Under scrutiny	Coming at me	Equal partnership
Bad things will happen	Bad things might happen	Good things might happen

Wherever you find yourself on this spectrum, it seems sensible that moving to the right towards a conversational interview mindset would seem to be more useful and, ultimately, ensure a better performance and result.

Conversations are interview practice

Most of us are naturally curious about one another, and so the more often you make use of the opportunity to talk about yourself – what you do, how you do it, your enthusiasms – the more likely you will find that interviews are just more of the same.

If I meet someone and ask them what they do, and they give me a dismissive or secretive answer – 'Oh, I just work for local government' – I'm disappointed. I think we can all practise conversational skills in these situations, so start doing this with other people – in a sensitive and non-interrogatory way, of course – and open up when other people do this to you. Get comfortable with the idea of talking about yourself, and help other people to do it, too.

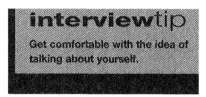

interviewtip

Get comfortable with the idea of talking about yourself.

Networking your way into a job

Most research into how people get jobs shows that very few people – perhaps as little as 10 per cent – get jobs through job adverts, but that up to 80 per cent of people get job offers through people they know and vague contacts – friends of friends and random meetings.

This spider's web of contacts and acquaintances is often referred to as a 'network'. By networking in a planned and deliberate way, you can open yourself up to surprising possibilities and job offers. So here's another reason to strike up conversations and enhance both your conversational and interview skills.

The fear-and-excitement continuum

We need to address the fear-factor aspect of interviews, but in the spirit of more productive and useful reframing (a new perspective on your interview mindset), consider the following definition maps:

FEAR MANIFESTATIONS	EXCITEMENT MANIFESTATIONS
Butterflies in stomach	Butterflies in stomach
Heart racing	Heart racing
Thoughts flying round brain	Thoughts flying round brain

I realise that this is as subtle as a punch in the face, but when you get fearful about a job, you call those manifestations 'fear', when you could just call them 'excitement'. In terms of interview preparation, you could be saying, 'I'm scared about this interview' or 'I'm excited about this interview.' Guess what psychologists have found? Your thinking or reframing can positively or negatively affect your performance in an interview. So that if you keep thinking something like this –

'Scared, scared, panic, terror – this will go badly!' (a **negative** thought loop)

it is likely to sabotage your performance. Whereas, if you were to practise thinking,

'This feeling I'm having could be excitement. I'm revving up for performance; this could be exhilarating!' (a **positive** thought loop)

you are more likely to perform at your optimum. There's more about this in Chapter 6, but what you need to realise is that it is only your perception of an event – how you think about it – that causes your feelings to surface. In short, you can control your feelings only if you control your thoughts.

However, it is worth analysing exactly what does concern (lose that 'fear' word!) you about interviews, so that you can plan to defuse them in the most powerful way. Take a moment to try the quiz below to identify your particular bugbears, and then we can start to distract these bears and tempt them to scoot off and leave you alone.

Quiz – What precisely scares you about interviews?
Go through this list of statements carefully and tick only those that exactly match your own experience. Be very selective, and don't worry if you don't tick one or two sections – just tick the statements that really match your feelings.

Section 1
☐ I'm not sure how to answer questions in the right way.
☐ Sometimes I'm not able to understand what the question is about.
☐ Sometimes I just don't understand the question.
☐ I seem to have trouble listening to the questions – they all become a blur.

I can't seem to gather my thoughts together so that I can explain what I mean.

I'm not sure how long to talk or how little to say.

I worry about my body language and what it is saying.

Section 2

I am never sure what to wear.

I want to be comfortable and don't know how I look best.

I want to look my best, but am not sure what this is.

I want them to look beyond the surface, but realise my appearance might get in the way.

Section 3

I don't like meeting new people.

I find it difficult to get to know people.

I find artificial situations tense.

I don't find it easy to talk to strange people.

Section 4

I don't like being tested.

I don't enjoy the idea of someone judging me.

I don't think it's fair that my ability to do the job is measured by my performance in an interview.

Section 5

I get sweaty palms.

My mouth dries up and my lips stick together.

My stomach churns.

My heart beats faster.

I feel anxious and shaky.

What your ticks mean

Now it may be that your ticks are spread throughout all the sections, but check first which section has the most ticks and then read the analysis below. There will probably be two sections that come out with the most ticks, and these will represent your strongest concerns about interviews – the ones you need to deal with and defuse first.

Predominantly Section 1 ticks: communication anxiety

It seems that your main concerns are about your own ability to communicate and how it can be disrupted by the interview situation. You can talk normally – you do this every day – but something about the artificiality of the situation trips you up. You also don't know what to expect – it's as if someone has dropped you on a strange planet without a map and everyone is talking some cryptic language.

WHAT TO DO

First of all, understanding what is going to happen during the interview – its format – will help you. Next, understanding the typical code language of an interview will make it all seem less alien. Chapter 3 will make this all seem simple. And as far as body language is concerned, the section on 'Let your body do the talking' in Chapter 4 will really enlighten you. Thorough preparation and knowing what to expect can deal with this particular bugbear, and a little time spent on ego stroking can do wonders (see Chapter 2).

Predominantly Section 2 ticks: appearance anxiety

Ticks in this section are to do with lack of confidence about your appearance – things like how fat/thin you are, how you look, what clothes are best to wear. Now the good news is that most interviewers barely notice what you look like unless there is something distracting about it – a loud tie, for instance, or jangly earrings. Much more important is your behaviour – how you hold yourself, standing and sitting, the expressions on your face and so on. As long as your clothes are neat and clean, your shoes polished, and the thoughts that show on your face and in your body language seem positive, nothing else will matter.

You cannot discount this, and if it seems a strange idea to you then you need to educate yourself soundly on this topic. You can do this in Chapter 4, where the subject of dress code for interviews is also covered.

interviewtip

As long as your clothes are neat and clean, your shoes polished, and the thoughts that show on your face and in your body language seem positive, nothing else will matter.

Other than that, just be certain that, despite appearances – yes, I mean **despite appearances** – employers want to find out what you can do for them. How you look and what you wear are less likely to influence them than your unique capabilities. Good image and appearance will help, of course, but getting hung up about it won't.

Predominantly Section 3 ticks: social anxiety

Some of us find social situations a little unnerving. If you hate the idea of walking into a crowded room full of strangers, then you belong to the 'I only like people I know' club, of which most of us are paid-up members. Add to this the fact that there are certain rules and courtesies common to these situations, which can make it all seem a bit confusing. Interviewees have to walk into an unfamiliar setting, talk confidently with complete strangers, and impress them at the same time. It is not surprising that phrases such as 'walking into a lion's den' spring to mind.

WHAT TO DO

All this may make you think of someone crossing a minefield, which does nothing to help you be easy in this situation. To help you soothe your anxieties a little on this score, it's worth considering the following –

- The people you like and know now were once strangers, so strangers are simply people you don't know – yet!
- Social courtesies are easy to learn and are a comforting framework for nervy situations (see Chapter 4).
- Most people find that when they feel nervous, **acting as if you are confident** works well – this isn't fake, it is a way of being resourceful (see Chapter 6).
- Finally, if you use a metaphor like a minefield or lion's den when thinking about an interview, you are just cranking up the anxiety quotient. It is far better to defuse the anxiety by finding a more neutral or objective metaphor, such as 'It's just a walk in the park with some people I don't know yet.'

Predominantly Section 4 ticks: performance anxiety

Interviews are a short cut to getting to know you, and interviewers have to use what are often crude and imperfect measures – the questions – to find out what they need to know in the shortest amount of time. It's this measuring and judging that seems to unnerve people. There is a sense that all questions are there to trick us into foolishness and failure. It is not exactly the performing itself that scares us, but rather that our performance won't convince and we will fail.

WHAT TO DO

The best antidotes to fear of failure and performing are the following:

- You have to have an unshakeable belief that what the interviewer perceives, or more than likely guesses, about you is probably just a shot in the dark that cannot really be the measure of you or your performance. All the same, it is your job to tempt them into making a more favourable guess (see Chapters 4, 5 and 6).
- Unshakeable self-belief in itself is the best antidote, and this is something that can be developed and encouraged by new ways of thinking. This does not mean that you should embrace arrogance and big-headedness, but that you accept yourself as a fully grown human being with strengths and unique qualities that an interviewer is longing to hear about.
- Rehearsal techniques and interview practice can make the strange familiar (see Chapter 6).
- Objective feedback can turn one bad interview into the next successful one (see Chapter 5).

Predominantly Section 5 ticks: behaviour anxiety

This may seem to overlap with social anxiety, and indeed they do often go together. But here we are specifically talking about the physical manifestations of interview fears – the dry mouth and shaking hands and any other physical symptoms of stress. Now, as these are almost directly related to your panicky thoughts about how badly things will go, learning to control your thoughts will promote calmness and focus. Techniques to master your thoughts and behaviour are covered in Chapter 6.

Mantras to defuse interview concerns

So now you should have a better idea of what makes interviews weird and stressful. You need to know this so precisely because once you know what the obstacles really are, you are on track to overcoming them. You can be sure that most people experience one or more of these anxieties about interviews, and just because they are so common, we can conclude that they cannot be insurmountable – you can do something about them. In fact, now we've uncovered them and exposed them to the clear and penetrating light of day, they can begin to seem rather insignificant – and that's how they need to stay!

A mantra is a yogic word sequence that can be repeated mentally and which can calm the mind and train thoughts. Try out the following mantras. They will implant new thought patterns to help you boost your confidence for interviews.

Interviews are just conversations in disguise.

Fear and excitement feel much the same.

Strangers are just people I don't know yet.

Thoughts show on my face and in my body language so to send positive signals, I need to control and train my thoughts.

chapter

2

Just who do you think you are?

You're in one of those scary survival situations. You and some friends find yourselves trapped on a mountainside with various challenging factors to deal with: the weather has changed dramatically; the mist is drawing in; the temperature is dropping; someone has slipped and sprained an ankle; there is no reception on anyone's mobile. It seems that you might have to spend the night on the mountain. Decisions have to be made.

Consider the three candidates for leadership in this situation:

1 Confident and positive: someone who takes a strong and positive lead, saying what she would do and delegating tasks, for example 'What we need to do here is …' or 'I can do … '

2 Hesitant: someone who says 'I'm wondering whether …' or 'I think I can …'

3 Silent and mostly unforthcoming: someone who says 'I'm not too bad at …' or 'I might be able to …'

Now, Candidate A might be able to persuade us of her suitability just through her sheer self-confidence and manner, although there is always the danger that she may not actually be able to do the things she is boasting about. Candidate B might be hesitant but still quite capable. Candidate C might be modest and unassuming but capable.

Nonetheless, in survival situations, you might not take the risk of picking B or C, both of whom might seem a bit of a gamble, but choose A just because she **seems** to be the most confident. You might not have time or the luxury of trying out the other two first.

Recruiters who interview for new employees find themselves in a very similar situation. They are generally impressed by someone who can say 'I can do …' and 'I find I'm good at …'. Most applicants make the mistake of hiding their light under a bushel, so to

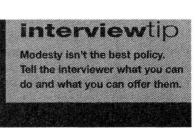

speak. Light hiders expect interviewers to be mind readers who can guess what they are capable of.

If you are something of a light hider, then you might be thinking that by saying, 'I am good at ...', you will sound boastful. This is a common mistake. Reluctance to tell an interviewer what you can do for them and what you can offer them results in recruiters going for people who are prepared to 'sell' themselves.

Selling yourself and boasting

We are almost programmed to dislike words and phrases like the ones above. We are brought up to be modest and are frequently told not to show off. This has a peculiar effect – many people will happily say they are not good at something or just OK at something even if the opposite is true.

This kind of false modesty is quite simply dishonesty. If you consider yourself too honest for good interview performance, then it is more than likely because you are loath to 'sell' yourself. In fact, selling yourself is quite honest, if that means helping the employer know just what you can offer them. Some gadgets sell themselves – they have good packaging and the instructions are on the box. We human beings might have good packaging (see Chapter 4), but there are no visible instructions. Selling yourself or promoting yourself is just your chance to help recruiters get past the packaging.

The time and luxury to pick the right person

In survival situations, there is no time to investigate who is the best person, and so **volunteered information and a declaration of skills** make us confident about who can lead.

Interviewers dream of candidates who will volunteer information and declare their skills, mostly so that interviews are not too time-consuming and so that selection of suitable employees goes smoothly. If you plan to win at interviews, you need to learn to

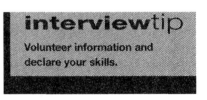

interviewtip

Volunteer information and declare your skills.

volunteer the most useful information and make a strong and proud declaration of your skills.

Grand and unjustifiable claims

This doesn't, of course, mean that you can make claims for abilities and experience that cannot be backed up. What it does mean is that for every wonderful quality or skill you mention, you can offer **evidence** to support the claim. Here's how it might go –

'I am extremely well organised and can work to deadlines – for example, in my current part-time job in a fast-food restaurant, we have targets to work to, including customer-service guidelines, and I have won the employee of the month award.'

interviewtip

Always offer evidence to back up your claims.

Using the phrase 'for example' is vital to make any volunteered information or declared skills real and convincing.

Three of the most common interview questions

If you consider the three most common interview questions, you can see how important it is not only to be able to promote your own skills and suitability for the job, but also to **know** what it is you have got beneath your packaging. Here are those three questions:

* Tell us about yourself.
* What do you have to offer us?
* Why should we employ you?

The phrasing of these questions might vary slightly, but versions of each or all of them pop up at most interviews. Instead of 'Tell us about yourself', the interviewer might ask, 'What is your previous experience?' or, 'How would you describe yourself?' (More in-depth advice about questions can be found in Chapter 8.)

Now can you guess the subtext or theme behind these questions?

The answer is that they all require you to have a clear idea of yourself and an idea of how your personal skills and qualities will match their requirements. To be able to do this, you have first to work out a personal profile – a description of your qualities, skills and experience.

The blurb – the instructions on the box

You're in the gadget store and there are lots of gadgets, all of which seem to be pretty much the same. You have to read the blurb and the instructions – what might be called the specification, or 'spec', which helps you decide which one to buy.

Applicants who get shortlisted for interviews are often very similar, and interviewers have to uncover what is special about each person. Good interviewers ask questions that help discover who you are and what you can offer. If, however, you don't have the answer to a simple question such as 'Describe yourself', you will look at best unperceptive and at worst foolish. You need to decide on your own blurb, so interviewers can get beyond your packaging.

I'm going to ask you to create your own blurb – what is often referred to as a 'self-marketing statement' – and it is going to be made up of four key categories: your personality qualities, your skills, your experience and your qualifications. Each category needs to be carefully considered so as to present a full and rounded statement.

Personality qualities and skills audit

These can be positive or what might seem to be negative qualities. Start by finishing off the following sentences with your own considered opinions on how you view yourself:

I am ... ─────────────────────────────────

(e.g. happy, quiet, shy, confident, capable, motivated, fun, reliable, outgoing, sociable, sensible, resourceful, calm, excitable).

I can be ... ─────────────────────────────────

(use any words that come to mind).

My best quality is ... ─────────────────────────────────

(e.g. my sense of humour, my honesty, my kindness, my enthusiasm).

My best skills are ... ─────────────────────────────────

(pick three skills, e.g. communication, interpersonal, listening, organisational, planning, analytical, teamwork, working to deadlines, leadership, sporting, artistic, creative, scientific, computer).

Experience and qualifications

Think back on your life experience including any experience of work, voluntary activities or travel. What did these experiences teach you? What did you gain from them? What can you do now as a result of these experiences? For example, if you spent a gap year in New Zealand, what sort of emergencies did you cope with and how did you manage them? Even the most mundane job can offer new skills and abilities. Take a look at the following case study.

Ayesha

Ayesha worked one student vacation in a hospital as a cleaner. She cleaned toilets and talked to patients. She also had responsibility for the operating theatre areas and hung curtains in the mortuary, which was a little weird because of the fridges and the dead bodies.

She gained –

■ proof of her ability to work in a team and with patients
■ evidence of being able to be sensitive and take
   responsibility.

case study

Now try and fill in the grid below with the information you have gathered from the self-audit.

Self-audit grid – write your own blurb			
Personality qualities	Skills	Experience	Qualifications

If you have really worked at this exercise thoroughly, you are halfway to answering the most common questions in most interviews. Here's how it works. Below is a completed grid for Ethan, a 16-year-old who was about to go for an interview for a modern apprenticeship in hospitality and catering as a chef.

Ethan's self-audit grid			
Personality qualities	Skills	Experience	Qualifications
Happy	Teamwork (school football)	Saturday job in cycle shop	GCSEs
Sense of humour	People skills (part-time job in retail)	School work experience in a cafe	First-aid certificate (Scouts)
Reliable	Practical (bike mending)	Paper round at 13	Food Technology award in Year 11
Organised (school coursework on time)			

Notice how Ethan has given himself a memory jogger of evidence ('for example', remember!) to prove the skills, qualities and experience he has recorded.

The three Es

Most employers admit to looking for three key selling points from applicants at interview. These are –

1 ENTHUSIASM

2 EMPLOYABILITY

3 EVIDENCE

Enthusiasm

However much self-analysis you have done and however clear you are about what your best qualities and skills are, it is how you put these across that counts. Imagine Ethan saying in a robotic, toneless voice: 'I am happy and reliable and have people skills from my part-time job.' Now imagine him saying it in an enthusiastic voice, as if were really true and real.

Enthusiasm is vital, and nothing is easier than adding enthusiasm through the use of intonation – that is, by projecting your voice and varying its tone (see Chapter 4) – and by adding small 'power' words interspersed in your sentences. Try the following:

'I *really* enjoy playing football,' instead of 'I play football.'

'I *love* meeting people,' instead of 'I like people.'

Just the addition of words such as 'really' and 'love' juice up the sentences to make you sound more enthusiastic.

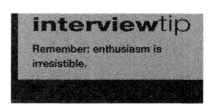

interviewtip

Remember: enthusiasm is irresistible.

Employability

This may seem an odd word, but by this employers mean that they want to know how employable you are; that is, how useful you can be to them. The following is a list of the most important employability characteristics that employers look for. Why not use this as a checklist for your own selling points? Go through the list and tick those that you believe you possess, and then come up with a 'for example' piece of evidence you could use to prove that you are not just making a bogus claim.

What employers want from you – how can you prove it?		
Employability characteristic (in order of importance)	**Tick here if you think you possess this.**	**The proof – write a statement.**
Willingness to learn		
Commitment		
Dependability/reliability		
Self-motivation		
Teamwork		
Communication skills (spoken and written)		
Drive/energy		
Self-management		
Achievement orientation/ motivation		
Problem-solving skills		
Analytical ability		
Flexibility		

Employability characteristic (in order of importance)	Tick here if you think you possess this.	The proof – write a statement.
Initiative		
Ability to summarise key issues		
Logical ability		
Adaptability		
Numerical skills		
Ability to work under pressure		
Time management		
Research skills		
Self-confidence		

The intention of this list is not to make you feel inadequate – no one is expected to have the full package of characteristics – but you should be able to pick out five or six from the list that you can really claim to possess. Below is an analysis of one person's self-analysis using the above table, which he used as a checklist to prepare for an interview. I have shown only the boxes he ticked, along with his 'for example' evidence.

Luke's self-analysis

Luke's package of skills and abilities	Tick here if you think you possess this.	The proof – write a 'for example' statement.
Willingness to learn	✓	I chose to study additional courses while at college, alongside my A-level study, to broaden out my abilities in computing (e.g. Dreamweaver web design).

Dependability/reliability	✓	I have worked at a paper shop for the last 3 years, starting at 5am to mark up the papers for delivery.
Teamwork	✓	I play football for local and college teams and have been club secretary, which involves collecting subs and arranging fixtures.
Ability to work under pressure	✓	I have completed my college study while holding down two part-time jobs.
Time management	✓	Coursework for most subjects I study involves research, which I have to fit in between my part-time jobs, my lessons and playing football for the college team in away and home competitions – this needs careful planning.

Remember that while the self-audit grid can help you answer the 'Tell me about yourself' and 'What can you offer?' questions, the 'Why should we employ you?' question is about employability characteristics. Looking down the employability characteristics list will give you some ideas of your own unique selling points. See Chapter 8 for more on interview questions and Chapter 5 for more on 'unique selling points', or USPs.

While making a winning interview is about matching yourself to the employer's requirements (see Chapter 5), you won't be convincing unless you are consistent. Being consistent means that you come across in a way that is ultimately truthful and honest – that when you say, 'I am really keen to work for you', this is convincing because of the way you say it and because it fits with your own requirements and career plan.

interviewtip

To be convincing, go for jobs that fit your requirements and your career plan.

It is probably a waste of time going for jobs that really don't interest you at all because this will be apparent when you answer the interview questions. That doesn't mean that every job you go for has to be the job of your dreams, but it is useful to go for jobs that look like taking you at least some way in the direction you want to go. Take a look at Consistent Caroline and Inconsistent Ilya.

Caroline

Consistent Caroline went for a job in a call centre, which involved some sales work and customer service. She wanted eventually to work for the health service as an occupational therapist, working with elderly patients. She was keen to work in a call centre because –

- it paid well and was flexible
- she could develop her skills of persuasion through the sales work
- sales work could teach her to deal with rejection
- talking to many different people would develop her communication skills.

It was consistent for Caroline to be enthusiastic about this work because it fitted with her own future career plans.

Ilya

Inconsistent Ilya went for an interview in a library for Saturday work. Eventually, he wanted to work on cruise liners as an entertainer. He didn't really like books and had quite a loud voice. At interview, he said he wanted to work in a library, but when asked why, he was stumped.

Knowing your own career plan

This is something that you might find a little perplexing. Some people have a very definite idea of how they want their future career to be; others are much more vague about this. Some people don't like to have a plan at all. Although it's not vital to have a fixed idea of where you want to be in a few years, it does help if you take the time to research the job market – what I call the 'What's out there' factor.

What's out there

If you have done a decent self-audit, you've started on the 'What's in here' bit. Ideally, good career planning is founded on the following formula –

**WHAT'S IN HERE + WHAT'S OUT THERE =
A FULFILLING AND HAPPY LIFE**

What this means is that knowing yourself (what's in here) means that you can really assess what is available for you (what's out there) and make a conscious, reasoned decision on what you need to make your life meaningful. Most people fall into careers and jobs by chance or through not knowing what is available to them. It's as if they have gone into a restaurant and have been given a menu with just two options. To access the full menu, you need to research what is available. Here's how.

Local/national newspapers' jobs sections

Take a look at what is being advertised and where. Send off for details of job adverts that interest you. Phone people up and ask for information. Find out what they are looking for and what you would have to do to be a credible applicant.

Web research

Put 'jobs and careers' into any search engine and career sites and recruitment agencies will come up, with a myriad of careers and jobs to entice you. Try the following as well:

- North West Students and Graduates On Line – www.nwsago.co.uk
- Prospects (for graduate careers) – www.prospects.ac.uk
- Springboard – www.springboard.co.uk
- Worktrain – www.worktrain.gov.uk

Connexions

If you're between 13 and 19 years of age, book some time with a Connexions Personal Adviser to discuss your ideas and where these might take you.

College and University Careers Advisers

Check with your local college or universities to see what careers advice might be available.

And finally ...

And finally, remember that it is pointless to go for a job interview unless it really fits with where you want your life to go. You won't be able to be convincing in an interview unless, in your heart of hearts, the job feels right to you.

So let's move on to an in-depth look at interviews and what really goes on in them.

3

The interview format – What's really going on

It may be that you are new to interviews and have no idea what to expect, or it may be you're reading this book because you have a little experience and that little was not particularly enjoyable. It may even be the case that all the interviews you've had so far have gone well, but that you expect higher-level job interviews to crank up the pressure. Whichever your situation, it's important to grasp the basic fact that behind every interview, regardless of the career or job area, there is a structure, or format, lurking. But don't worry! A format is just a way for employers to be sure that interviews cover the right ground and actually finish within a reasonable amount of time.

Employer daydreams

Most interviews begin as an idea in the head of a recruiter or employer some time before the interview takes place. They start almost as a kind of employer's daydream that goes something like this:

'We seem to be really busy and we need some help with the filing … If we took someone on they could also answer the phones, and if they had some web skills they could do some work on the website … they could even mailshot our customers with special offers.'

After some thinking and discussion, a job profile is created, reflecting the idea that the employer has imagined of the ideal applicant. In this dreamy period, other details might be added, such as how much they might have to pay this ideal person and what experience/qualifications might show that this person could do the job.

The next stage

A job advert and often a detailed job specification are created, and that's when real people become interested in the job, applying by application form or CV. Details are sent out to applicants who express an interest by phoning or writing to the employer. Occasionally the only details available are those that appear in the, often mysterious, job advert, so this means that applicants have to guess what the employer is looking for.

Quite often this stage can be a shock for the employer, who may find that the ideal applicant is not easy to find. She or he trawls through application forms and CVs and often becomes despondent because that ideal is not accurately matched in the applicants who have shown an interest. This can be the fault of the job advert, the salary being offered, the timing of the recruitment or just because there is a shortage of people available with the skills and experience required.

Most of the time, though, applicants have simply misread or misinterpreted the advert and job spec, and this results in their application being quite off-target in terms of matching the employer's expectations. The only way to avoid this happening is to make a detailed analysis of the job advert and/or spec, and match your application ruthlessly to the hidden or stated requirements (there's more on this below).

Shortlisting and longlisting

Imagine you're an employer or human-resource (HR) professional with a huge pile of CVs or application forms. On average, an advert in a national newspaper can generate hundreds of applications; even local newspaper adverts can result in similar quantities.

You have to start by whittling down the pile, so you take out those that seem messy or unprofessional. Then you start scanning those left, putting some on the 'definite' pile, some on the 'possible' pile and some on the 'bin it' or rejection pile.

You might then have a 'longlist' of thirty or so, and you think you want to interview between eight and ten applicants over two days. So you start again, reminding yourself of your key requirements. You read through the applications with one vital and objective thing in mind: how convincingly has each applicant shown that he or she has every single thing I want and have asked for in my job advert/spec?

Most recruiters will methodically and brutally match an application against each and every requirement of the job and tick against these criteria. The criteria – what they asked for – might be 'essential' or 'desirable'.

Essential or desirable

In simple terms, the essential criteria are what the employer believes are the 'must-haves' for the job. For example, a job advert might say: 'Must have at least four GCSEs at C grade and over, including Maths and English,' or 'Must have experience of Visual Basic.'

If an applicant has all the essential criteria, then he or she will probably make the first longlist – the 'possible' pile. If a lot of applicants have these essential requirements, then the recruiter will pick out those who have the desirable criteria, too – the 'added-value' extras they are hoping for and which they clearly requested in their job spec.

Under desirable criteria, the job spec might, for example, state 'Knowledge of Microsoft Excel would be an advantage' – they are not saying 'Must have Microsoft Excel', but they would be interested in an applicant who could offer this as an added-value extra.

Sometimes these desirable criteria will be clearly requested in the job spec or description under a helpful heading, which, you've guessed it, will read 'Desirable criteria', or just 'Desirable'. At other times, however, these added-value extras will be hinted at, and you will need to read between the lines to take the hint!

What this means for you

Analyse the job advert and job spec (learn how to do this in Chapter 5), make a list of the essential and desirable criteria, both obvious and hidden (good employers do this for you in their application guidelines), and then customise your CV and application form to what is being requested.

Sadly, most applications do not pull off this simple trick – they often respond by mismatching what the employer has generally **strictly and exactly** asked for. Here's a way to imagine it – you go to a shop wanting to buy an iron, and you describe exactly what you want in great detail:

Worst-scenario application

Here's an example of a well-meaning but wildly mismatched application.

case study

Cara

Cara saw a job advert for a fork-lift truck driver. It was clear that any applicants should possess three clear abilities:

- A fork-lift licence
- Perfect eyesight
- Experience of warehouse work.

Cara wanted to be a lorry driver and applied for this job in the hope that she could move on to that kind of work. In her letter of application, she wrote,

'I am very keen to apply for the role of fork-lift truck driver and would eventually like to move into big-truck driving. I can offer reliability and a strong interest in warehouse work. Even though I do not have experience of this role, I am willing to learn.'

If you were a reasonable employer, you could be forgiven for wondering the following –

- 'If I did offer her a job as a fork-lift truck driver, how long will she do it before becoming a lorry driver?'
- 'Does she have perfect eyesight and forget to mention it?'
- 'It's nice that she is interested in warehouse work, but it would seem that she has no licence to drive a fork lift and is expecting me to pay for her to learn.'

Most employers would be exasperated by this well-meaning but vague application, which does nothing to prove that Cara would be the best person for the job.

Pretty bad scenario

interviewtip

If you do not meet every one of the expressed or suggested essential criteria for the job, it will be a waste of time applying for it – spare yourself the bother. Essential means essential in job adverts and specs.

Just like the customer who goes to buy an iron, the employer is sometimes unconvinced by out-of-date qualifications or experience. Here's an example:

Jack

Jack had worked for two weeks' work experience at a photography shop when he was 15. A few years later, he applied for a job in a photo lab. While this past experience was worth mentioning, with changes in the photographic industry such as the development of digital photography, more recent experience was required. If he relied on this old experience totally, an employer could be unconvinced. This is what he did instead – here is a portion of his covering letter, which accompanied his CV:

'My interest in photography began as a hobby and was strengthened through membership of my school and college photography clubs – this was the reason for my choice of work experience in a photography shop. Since then I have constantly updated my skills and experience through personal interest and through the use of digital packages on my current media-studies course.'

Jack nailed this application with the evidence of his enthusiasm and his experience, while allaying any worries an employer might have had about the currency of his skills.

For more information and details about CVs and cover letters, have a look at my *Winning CVs for First-time Job Hunters* in this series (published by Trotman).

The final, still-bad scenario – the iron you didn't want

When an applicant appears to wilfully ignore the exact requirements and offer something which might seem vaguely similar but is fact quite the opposite to the declared criteria, it makes some recruiters want to scream and shout, 'That's not what I want – that's not what I said I wanted!'

So the answer is this:

Read what the job advert or spec says or suggests carefully. Analyse it rigorously. Analyse exactly how you can match the requirements – then tell the employer exactly how you match every single line of their job description and then, if you really want to impress, show them your added value (that you match their desirables; there's more about this in Chapter 5).

interviewtip

Read the job advert carefully. Tell the employer how you match every single line of their job description.

You're on the shortlist and are sent an interview invitation

Job rejections can be about five to ten times as frequent as interview invitations, so that invitation letter plopping down onto your mat can seem like the finishing line, the successful outcome ... If only!

Now the work really starts. There should be information about the interview timetable in the letter – that is, an idea of how it will go and whether you will be required to bring anything or give a presentation. This is when you move into full preparation mode, which is covered in Chapter 5.

The day of the interview – the normal format

1 You arrive and you greet and are greeted.

2 You wait somewhere and wonder what will happen.

3 You walk in and sit down in front of the interviewer or the panel of interviewers.

4 The main interviewer or the chair of the panel explains the background to the role and the purpose of the interview.

5 An icebreaker question or two.

6 Some general 'finding out about you and your motivation for the job' questions.

7 Specific questions that seek to discover how you would measure up in the role.

8 Situational questions.

9 Your chance to ask questions.

10 Wrapping up the conversation/interview.

Now all this may seem rather obvious. However, in the spirit of overdosing on information about interviews as a way of guarding against interview nerves, the next chapters will deal with every single detail behind the typical interview format. Just to get you thinking, read each statement below and work out which stage of the interview they are from.

Quiz – Which bit of the interview is this?

'Well, Hannah – we've asked all our questions; what would you like to know about the job?'

'We'd be interested if you could tell us why you applied for this job.'

'How do you deal with angry customers?'

'I wonder what they're doing in there and when they will call me in.'

'Did you come by bus or did you drive here?'

'What specifically interests you about this job?'

'We want someone who can come up with ideas and see projects through – why should we employ you?'

'You found us all right, then?'

'Tell us about yourself and your previous experience.'

'What would people who know you say are your main qualities or characteristics?'

'How much experience do you have of using Quark Xpress?'

'Tell me about a time when you had to stay calm in a crisis.'

'What can you offer us?'

'The job role as I see it is about providing technical support and advice to our administrative staff, and we need to recruit someone with the right skills and experience.'

'I'm interested in knowing whether there is any further training you would like me to undertake.'

'Tell us why you think you are the right person for this job.'

'When will I hear your decision?'

Here are the answers to the quiz, shown as statements and questions and in the right sequence. So how did you do?

Interview format with typical questions

'I wonder what they're doing in there and when they will call me in.' (Applicant's normal anxiety)

'Did you come by bus or did you drive here?' (Icebreaker)

'You found us all right, then?' (Icebreaker)

'The job role as I see it is about providing technical support and advice to our administrative staff, and we need to recruit someone with the right skills and experience.' (Employer explains the role and purpose.)

'Tell us about yourself and your previous experience.' (General question)

'We'd be interested if you could tell us why you applied for this job.' (General question becoming specific)

'What specifically interests you about this job?' (General question becoming specific)

'What would people who know you say are your main qualities or characteristics?' (General question becoming specific)

'Tell us why you think you are the right person for this job.' (Specific question)

'What can you offer us?' (Specific question)

'How do you deal with angry customers?' (Specific question)

'Tell me about a time when you had to stay calm in a crisis.' (Very specific and situational question)

'We want someone who can come up with ideas and see projects through – why should we employ you?' (Very specific, prove-yourself-to-us question)

'How much experience do you have of using Quark Xpress?' (Very specific question)

'Well, Hannah – we've asked all our questions; what would you like to know about the job?' (Wrap up)

'I'm interested in knowing whether there is any further training you would like me to undertake.' (Applicant questions)

'When will I hear your decision?' (Applicant questions)

If you're wondering how to deal with the intricacies of answering the questions above, then Chapter 8 covers this in detail, including the code language often used in interviews – those strange words and phrases that can perplex and mystify.

Understanding what to expect is really half the battle – it's often the uncertainty, the interview territory being unknown, that causes negative thoughts to surface. So now that the territory seems a little more familiar, we can move on to consider how you can cultivate your image to help you make the best interview impression.

Making an impact with the right image

You meet someone for the first time. How long, would you guess, does it take you to decide whether you like them or not? When this someone is speaking to you, what influences you most? Their clothes, their hairstyle, their age or sex, their choice of words or how clever they sound, their accent, their tone or pace of their speaking; or something almost indefinable, such as how they stand or look at you or how they use their hands when they are speaking?

Serious research into first impressions and communication in the 1970s by a man named Albert Mehrabian showed that making an impact is much more complex and fascinating than simply the clothes we wear. In fact, surface details such as what we wear, while important, are less important than the subconscious clues that leak out of us when we meet someone for the first time.

This 'leakage', often referred to as body language, might summon up images of alien goo or the Creature from the Black Lagoon, and you might be wondering what exactly is leaking out!

It's worth thinking about a time when perhaps you asked a friend, 'Hey, did you have a good weekend?' and they might have said, 'Yeah!', but you just had a sense that what they really meant was that it hadn't been a good weekend at all.

What you were picking up on were the conflicting signals they were transmitting. It's a bit like a badly tuned radio – you can hear one piece of music with another one from another station merging in. It's confusing – there seems to be one signal and then another one beneath it or even on top of it.

Now, we often find it easier to pretend we are happy or have had a happy time rather than be quizzed about a less-than-happy experience. We might have had a row with someone over the weekend and still be feeling sad or weepy and unwilling to talk about it, so we say, 'Yeah, I had a good weekend,' because we don't want to get into it. The point is that invariably the feelings that conflict with our words leak out in our tone of voice and in our posture. Normally, if we had had a good weekend, we would say 'Yeah' in an upbeat tone and our posture would be relaxed and open. If, in fact, we had a miserable weekend, our tone will seem low and lifeless and our posture might be hunched and tense.

So it's worth taking some time to really get to grips with what first impressions are about, so that you know how to make the most of that first 30 seconds or so in an interview and make a real difference to an interviewer's opinion of you.

The 30-second window

Interviewers admit that they are influenced by the first few minutes, although good interviewers will try to be as objective as possible, so that they check for evidence of your suitability and ignore first impressions if they seem too unreasonable.

Nonetheless, it's useful to focus on the first few minutes and maximise your chance of making that good first impression. The first 30 seconds particularly is a window of opportunity for you and, amazingly, it's less about whether you can do the job than how confidently you come across as you walk in and sit down and perhaps deal with the first question. You probably have some ideas about what is going on in those first seconds, so try the following quiz to check out just how much you know. Decide on true or false for the following statements –

QUIZ – LET YOUR BODY DO THE TALKING

Body language sign	Good/Bad
Walking into interview not knowing where to look	
Hands together lightly and loosely	
Leaning forward in seat	
Shoulders alert	
Sitting back in chair	
Eyes constantly fixed on interviewer	
Hands clasped firmly	
Light, warm tone	
Bag in one hand, folder in the other	
Lips together in a fixed expression	

Steady and gentle eye contact

Looking up and away for long periods while thinking of an answer

Folded arms

Walking in and focusing on interviewer

Use of hands when talking

Sitting on edge of seat

Handshake and smile

Flat tone of voice

Wandering eyes

Introduce yourself by name

Shaking hands while looking at clasped hands

Walking in looking down

Shoulders slightly back and dropped down

First let's have the answers. The shaded rows are all believed to be powerful signs of confidence and readiness for the interview situation and are, therefore, key techniques for you to focus on, especially if you do these roughly in the right order, something like this:

The ten perfect body-language signs
Introduce yourself by name
Handshake and smile
Walking in and focusing on interviewer
Steady and gentle eye contact
Light, warm tone
Sitting back in chair
Shoulders slightly back and dropped down
Hands together lightly and loosely
Use of hands when talking
Gently allow your gaze to brush over the panel of interviewers

Now, the key body-language signals group themselves into four convenient categories:

1 EYES

2 HANDS

3 POSTURE

4 VOICE

So let's examine these.

Eye signs

First impressions are mainly visual and so interviewers make lightning observations of the whole you that appears through the door, but as soon as your eyes look at theirs, a contact is made – think of it like two wires connecting. You have to make the most of this by gently making eye contact with the interviewer or, if there is a panel, by brushing your eyes over the panel members. Here is the crucial thing you must do at the same time – **SMILE** – and if there is an opportunity reach out and offer your hand to shake.

interviewtip

Make eye contact, smile and shake hands.

The eye contact on its own is virtually worthless and possibly aggressive if you just look at them. By focusing on them, smiling at them and offering your hand, you are initiating a relationship in a confident way that says, ' I am confident and taking a little bit of control in this odd situation.'

FIXED EYES, WANDERING EYES AND EYES THAT LOOK UP/DOWN, ALL AROUND, WHEN QUESTIONED
Excessive eye contact and lack of eye contact are negative signs for most human beings and are often the sign of insecurity or a mental-health problem. You don't want to allow the wrong signal to go out about you. In the animal world, fixed eye contact is a sign of a predator or aggression and looking away is a sign of a victim or who will be next for dinner.

LOOK AWAY THINKING
Unfortunately our brains have a habit of making some of us look away under pressure of questioning, so we can think without the interviewer in our faces,

so to speak. This is an unconscious response which is natural, but what we do have to do after our brief 'look away thinking' is to re-establish eye contact, reconnect and then give our verbal response. Many people make the mistake of looking away to think of an answer, and then answering the question with their eyes fixed on some distant point on the horizon. This makes the interviewer feel abandoned and uncomfortable. Not a good thing to do!

Hand jives

The open-hand gesture of a handshake is one of the most powerful links we have with our cave-dwelling ancestors – by offering an open and empty hand, we are saying, 'I don't have a weapon in my hand – I come as a friend!'

Some people have been brought up to shake hands, and it comes naturally. If it doesn't feel natural, it's something you need to cultivate. As a general rule, the fingers of your hand should be pointing towards the other person, with your thumb raised. You should intend to 'bump' palms with them, while allowing your thumb to reach down to touch the outside of their hand.

Gripping just their finger in a half-hearted attempt will not do you any favours – often it hurts and it gives the impression that you don't really want to do this handshake thing. Practise first by handshaking yourself – I know this sounds odd, but you will get an idea of just the right pressure to exert!

Place your hands together as if you are just about to clap, then allow your hands to clasp each other without interweaving your fingers – the two thumbs should cross over naturally and all the fingers of the right hand should be touching the back of your left hand and vice versa. There is a lot of rubbish talked about handshakes but, as a general rule, a limp handshake is bad and an averagely firm handshake is good – just enough pressure to be convincing without causing the other person pain. Now practise this with other people – ask friends to practise and check what seems to be the best pressure. Do it enough to let it become normal and relaxed.

And finally, in handshake custom, it's generally good to be the first one to offer your hand; being proactive and assertive in this way sends out a good signal.

OTHER HAND MANOEUVRES

The next thing to consider is what you do with your hands in the interview. It is preferable to have one hand free to handshake, which is why having too much to carry will work against you, but once they are sitting ready for questions, most people find that placing their hands loosely in their lap, perhaps gently clasped, works well.

Try this now. Interweave your fingers in a firm clasp – you'll find that your arms and shoulders go tense with the effort.

Now ease off the pressure and slide your hands apart slightly until your shoulders drop down slightly and fingers are almost floppy but still touching. It will feel much better. Experiment with what feels easy and natural to you, but you will probably find that a gentle, loose clasp is best.

Believe it or not, anywhere else you choose to put your hands will probably cause you problems. Here are some examples:

What are you doing with your hands?

Location of hands	Sign
Hands waving about wildly	Distracting
Hands on the seat or slightly tucked beneath you	Something to hide
Hands/arms crossed	Making a barrier
Hands hanging by side	Distorts shoulders and posture
Hands touching face or mouth all the time	Something to hide

USING YOUR HANDS TO TALK

While wild gesticulating can be distracting to the interviewer, some gentle and regular use of the hands is highly recommended, but only if this is something that you are in the habit of doing.

Research has shown that use of your hands is a clear indication of your honesty and genuineness, so keep on doing it if it's what you normally do. (In fact, it has been found that when lying people find it hard to use their hands and talk at the same time.) If you do use your hands when chatting to friends, then it probably helps your flow of conversation, so it is important to do it in interviews if you want to appear relaxed and confident.

Otherwise, the best advice is to keep your hands mainly in front of you at

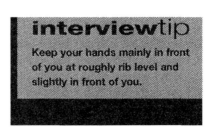

interviewtip

Keep your hands mainly in front of you at roughly rib level and slightly in front of you.

roughly rib level and slightly in front of you. Between questions, allow them to rest in your lap.

Posture and sitting up straight

This can be confusing because some posture experts maintain that sitting up straight with shoulders erect is what you need to do. I have to disagree with them.

Try this now. Sit up really straight. You'll find that your shoulders go up and feel like they could touch your ears and you make a sharp intake of breath. Now in this posture, try and say something. At worst, your voice will come out in a squeak; at best, it won't project very well.

Now from that constricted position, roll your shoulders back and down and take a deep breath that makes your belly fill out with air, from the bottom of your lungs pushing on your stomach. Take in a couple of breaths, in this position, allowing your shoulders to drop a little. Now push the bottom of your spine into the base of your chair and do the roll back and down shoulder sequence again and then the deep belly breaths. Now say something.

You will find that your voice can really project because your posture is allowing your lungs to breathe properly.

Whatever chair they give you, *always* push yourself back into the seat, allowing the chair to support the whole of your back, then do the shoulder roll back and down, then one belly breath, then look up at the interviewer, lock eyes gently and smile to indicate your readiness.

Maintain this posture throughout the interview. Practise it in other situations first – try it in class or in a doctor's waiting room – it really works!

Voice tricks

Your posture will have a big impact on how your voice projects, but there are some other tricks that can help you, too. Again, research into what good communication is shows that it is not *what* we say but *how* we say things that conveys our meaning. In fact, our tone and pace of voice plus our body language amount to 93 per cent of what we actually communicate. The words we use contribute only 7 per cent to our actual communication.

SO WHAT CAN YOU DO ABOUT YOUR TONALITY?

Think about a situation when you are with friends. You are all chatting, and there is probably warmth and excitement in your tone. The pace of your speech varies, with interesting pauses. When you ask questions or give answers, your voice will probably go up. There is a natural flow, which you may think is hard to put on in an interview.

It is not really about putting it on; it's more about letting it out! The oddness of an interview often makes us speak in a robotic or unnatural way. So remind yourself that this is just another conversation and use your own style, trusting yourself to drop into informal language such as 'OK' or 'That really gives me a buzz because' or 'I really love to ...' or 'No one ever asked me that before ... or 'I need to think about that one.'

Compare the two short interview excerpts below:

> **Scenario 1**
>
> Interviewer Tell us about your current job and what you like about it, please.
> Interviewee OK – well, I've been in this job role for about two years and just love the team I work with. We work well together and help each other out in busy periods. Mainly I am in charge of customer orders, chasing them up, making suppliers know that I am on the case, but I get a buzz when a customer knows they can trust me to make things happen for them.

> **Scenario 2**
>
> Interviewer Tell us about your current job and what you like about it.
> Interviewee I work in customer service and like the teamwork and doing the job properly so that the customer gets the service they deserve.

Now, the interviewee in Scenario 2 is not answering particularly badly, but she is a little stilted. The answer sounds almost like a formula, which does not necessarily show much enthusiasm. Scenario 1 shows an interviewee who is almost talking naturally; the use of words like 'buzz' and 'really' help make her intonation light and varied, instead of a monotone.

A monotone is a one-tone delivery – think of a robot – and often occurs when someone is nervous, trying to be something they're not or throwing off a practised, memorised answer.

Those of you who watch Australian soaps will have noticed that the Australian intonation has a tendency to go up at the end of sentences. This can be worth cultivating, as it gives a sense of eagerness in interviews. Try saying the following phrase in two different ways – first in a level tone as if you were reading it out, and then using emphasis on particular words and allowing your voice rise at the end of the sentence.

'I really want to progress in my career.'

STIFF-UPPER-LIP AND DRY-MOUTH SYNDROMES

Consciously allow your tongue to loll in your mouth and let your lips part slightly, and you'll find you're more ready to smile that if you have your lips pressed firmly together. Take a good drink of water before the interview and do a little gargle with it. This can help to relax your mouth to allow your voice to power through.

If you travel by car to your interview, sing loudly to your favourite CV in the car to warm your voice up – an interview is like a marathon for your voice, so give it some warm-up time.

PAUSES FOR EMPHASIS

The pace of your speaking is very important in interview, so practice pausing for emphasis, in mid-sentence or between phrases or sentences. Nerves often make us talk faster, so focus on a reasonable pace which is not too fast or too slow, but varied with faster sections followed with slower bits for real emphasis. Read the following section which is the answer to the interview question 'What do you have to offer our organisation?' and play around with the pace and emphasis.

> Interviewer   'What do you have to offer our organisation?'
> Interviewee 'Well, I have done this work before, so I know just what the
> challenges are. For this work, you need to be highly
> organised and able to work to targets. In my previous work,
> I organised the workload for a team of six and we exceeded
> our targets for contacts with clients. I pay attention to detail
> and like to plan my work, and I am competitive, so targets
> are great for me. Most importantly, I really want to work for
> your organisation, and I believe that in addition my
> Portuguese language skills will help you in the import/export
> contacts with that country.'

Here's an analysis of how this might have been delivered with emphasised words in bold, instructions about pauses and a critique of what was good about this answer in brackets.

> 'Well (small pause), I **have** done this work before, so I know **just** what the challenges are. (He is also saying – 'I'm OK with challenges'.) For this work (small pause), you need to be (pause) **highly** organised and able to work to targets (upward intonation). In my previous work, I organised the workload for a team of six and we **exceeded** our targets for contacts with clients. (Longer pause; he has shown evidence of his suitability.)
>
> 'I pay attention to detail (small pause) and like to plan my work, and I am competitive so targets are **great** for me. Most importantly (pause), I **really** want to work for your organisation, and I believe that in addition (pause) my Portuguese language skills will help you in the import/export contacts with that country.'

This is just an example, of course, and pauses and intonation could go differently, but it ought to give you an idea of how pace and flow can improve your voice projection.

Work inside your head

Most of this body language, or what is called non-verbal language, is below-the-surface stuff that comes out without us really being aware of it. Now you know about it you can be conscious of it and start practising techniques to rev up your non-verbal language skills to improve your confidence and how you come across. Nonetheless, both your confidence and image are mostly to do with how you are thinking about yourself and whether you really believe you are the right person for the job.

We all have random thoughts that career around our heads – generally these are reactions to what we see, hear or feel. Many of these are just fairly mindless wonderings, which can often turn up later in our dreams – we may see a wheelbarrow in a garden as we are walking along and, hey presto! – there is a wheelbarrow in our dream. You might not even think you had a wheelbarrow thought, but just noticing it causes a random thought, which your mind tries to tidy away at the end of the day in your sleep.

Other random thoughts are more harmful – you might think someone doesn't like you or has made a put-down remark. This kind of thought creates a kind of minefield of negative thoughts and feelings, which often show quite transparently on your face – that's what I'm calling leakage.

If you think the thought, 'That teacher hates me!', your face will show a negative leakage – a tightening of the mouth or eyes. In addition, your body might display tense shoulders or a hunched posture.

If you walk into an interview thinking, 'I probably won't get this job,' or, 'They're going to try and trip me up,' the negative vibe coming off you will be screeching, 'Don't employ me!'

Control your thoughts and you will control the leakage

It seems obvious that random thoughts may come and go, but you can direct your thoughts by saying –

'I am so right for this job,' or

'I know I can show them I am right for this job,'

and reverse any natural nervous tendencies by guarding against and defusing those negative thoughts.

You are using your powers of cognition (the thoughts you direct) to re-programme your own brain for more positive thinking and therefore more powerful non-verbal signals.

This really works and is covered more fully in Chapter 6, including a special technique called cognitive rehearsal which can help you rev up for the interview by using your thoughts to help you.

interviewtip

Control your thoughts and think positively.

Dressing for success

Something that is referred to as the 'halo effect' goes on in the first few minutes of the interview, and this sets the scene and tone of how the interview is likely to go. This is where awareness of leakage and body language play their part. Nonetheless, surface stuff like what you wear also has an impact on the image you create – the inside bit is the thinking you do and what comes; the outside bit is how you present yourself image-wise. This is, in fact, the easy bit.

General image rules

When asked about interview image, interviewers rarely remember the detail of what interviewees wear, but they do have an overall positive or negative impression. Here are the top tips from interviewers on what to wear.

> **What to wear**
> Dark suits for men
> Jacket and skirt or dress for women
> Some employers like women in trouser suits; some don't
> Polished lace-up shoes for men
> Polished medium-heel shoes for women
> Light-coloured shirts for men with bright but not wildly crazy tie
> Neat beards/moustaches for men or well-shaven appearance
> Simple jewellery for women
> Subtle but well-applied make-up for women
> Simple bag or briefcase
> Muted colours or one bright colour which suits skin tone

Interviewers dislike jangly earrings or any jewellery that distracts their attention. Similarly, loud cartoon ties are likely to cause a bad reaction. Most expect a formal look for interviews, but if the nature of the company is very informal, you may choose to go for a less formal look. It is always better to opt for a formal, smart look rather than look underdressed.

Mostly, you want to wear something that is comfortable and that will allow you to breathe, something that will not crease and stay smart – something, in short, which you can forget about.

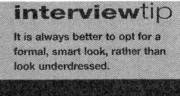

interviewtip

It is always better to opt for a formal, smart look, rather than look underdressed.

Remember, the overall impression you want to create is that you are smart (in all senses of the word) and capable. The clothes you choose are the armoury that protects and promotes you.

Finally, many interviewers mention that social courtesies such as handshakes, pleases and thank-yous impress. These are actually very easy to practise and cultivate. If you use these skills in the first few minutes, you have the chance of making a lasting first impression that will overcome anything that goes on in the later part of the interview, so let your body do the talking and your mouth can deal with the rest.

Optimum performance through in-depth preparation

Any performer will tell you that a performance takes practice and preparation. Performing at interview may sound like this is a false 'you' that has to be on show, but in fact it would be more precise to say that it's the best 'you' that needs to be on show – the best 'you' for that interview. Let me explain. We are all many different personalities under one skin. I'll describe someone so that you can get an idea of what I'm saying:

Sam plays rugby, and when he is with his rugby mates he is loud and energetic and sociable. When he works in his part-time job as a groundsman, he works with only one or two people or on his own. He is quiet and hard-working and just gets on with it. In his bar job, he is chatty and smiley and outgoing.

When he visits his gran, he is quite chatty but he listens a lot (she herself is quite a chatterer). On his journalism course he has a few good friends, but he has little time to socialise owing to his job and study commitments, so if you saw him you might see him being quieter, reading a lot and sitting in front of a computer. Sometimes he is a great socialiser, leading other people in events and activities; at other times he enjoys cooking or reading thrillers.

Sam has many aspects to his personality – which bits would be most interesting to an employer when interviewing? If he says he likes reading on his own or that he is quiet and a good listener, that might suit certain types of job, but if the job requires someone outgoing and sociable, then he needs to emphasise that side.

Similarly, we all have days when our hair looks weird or when we are wearing our old slippers and baggy clothes. If we are working from home doing Internet work or even telephone work, this probably won't matter, but we might pick a good hair-and-clothes day for other types of work.

Performing at interview is just about choosing what you want to let people know about you and showcasing that. If you are a trainspotter, this might be something you would mention at an interview for a rail company, but may be less useful for a job as a beauty therapist. So try and get comfortable with the idea of the interview as a chance to showcase yourself, with the performance being your selection of what you think they need to know. If you think of it this way, you will come across as authentic and smart.

Perfect preparation

Just like an actor preparing for a part, you will need to take some time to get yourself ready and in the right mindset to face the interview with calm confidence. That is your goal. A half-hour interview is intense, and if you go into it without preparation it would be like someone trying to run a marathon without coaching or training, so be ready to get in training.

The training regime

It's rather simple when you focus on it this way – it's made up of:

1 working out who you are and what you have to offer, and

2 working out who they are and what they have to offer.

You begin by choosing from all your amazing characteristics and decide which ones to let them – the employers – know about. They make it easy by giving you a list of what they want, and you can then match yourself against it. You may be thinking you have never seen a list of what they want, but I have mentioned this already when I talked about 'desirable' and 'essential' characteristics in Chapter 3. We are going to go deeper into this, by psychoanalysing a job advert. This will help you develop the skills you need to work out what you can offer them, according to what they have said they want.

Training regime Phase 1: Are you fit enough?

Any tool has to be fit for its purpose. In the same way, an employer wants to know whether you fit his or her job spec; that is, the purpose of that job role.

You can analyse a job advert, a job description or job spec/role (sent to you by the employer) in the same way. All you need to do is to pay attention to both the obviously expressed requirements for the job and the subtext in the copy (what they have written). The subtext is what seems to be hinted at in the job advert or job spec.

Look at the following job adverts and pick out what they are obviously stating and what they might be suggesting (the subtext).

Psychoanalyse some job adverts

Advert 1

GENERAL ASSISTANT FOR A PR AGENCY

An excellent way into PR and a great opportunity to join a successful agency.

Duties include general admin, post, correspondence, website maintenance and telephone work.

Essential skills – high level of computer literacy, 50wpm typing, accuracy, attention to detail, and the ability to prioritise. The ideal candidate will be a team player and have a good sense of humour.

Apply in writing to....

Your analysis –
Basic, obvious details

What is the objective, hard data they have put across?

The subtext (what is suggested)

Advert 2

EVENTS SUPPORT OFFICER FOR NATIONAL CHARITY

Salary up to ... NW London

To complement the team and support its development, we are looking for someone with a customer-service background who appreciates the importance of professional and proactive service.

You will have strong keyboard skills, competency in MS Word, a good telephone manner, the ability to work to deadlines and a friendly personality.

Please apply to ...

Your analysis –
Basic, obvious details

What is the objective, hard data they have put across?

The subtext (what is suggested)

Here's my analysis of both adverts – did you pick up all the clues?

Advert 1 has the obvious details such as 'general admin' and typing speeds – they are easy to pick up. The subtext is suggesting that they think this is a good career opportunity for someone, and they think they are quite a buzzy, exciting agency. They also want someone who is highly organised (accuracy, prioritise) and a bit of a perfectionist, or at least someone with high standards (attention to detail). Most importantly, they are suggesting that this would not suit a loner or someone who works best on their own, but it would suit someone who is perhaps bouncy and lively (team player/sense of humour).

From this kind of analysis, you can plan either the content of your application form or how you frame your CV – you will need to hit all the obvious and subtext buttons in anything you write about yourself. Similarly, you can virtually second-guess the questions they will need to ask you to find out if you suit their idea of the ideal candidate.

Advert 2 again gives the obvious details, clearly stated (MS Word/customer-service background), but offers a detailed subtext on what they really want. Words like 'complement' suggest the importance of team fit – they will be recruiting someone who fits into the existing team and can show a 'friendly personality'. You may not be able to guess what personalities make up the team, but if you could show that you are flexible, adaptable and easygoing, this might hit the right button for them. Words like 'professional' and 'proactive' are very strong clues to the ethos of this company, which is a charity and therefore will have certain standards of behaviour (professional), while at the same time requiring staff to be positive and promote the charity (proactive).

How did you find that exercise? You will certainly get better at this with practice, and it is an incredibly useful skill to develop. It is as if you are getting the chance to get inside the employer's mind – valuable preparation for any interview.

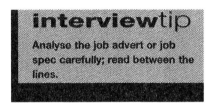

interviewtip

Analyse the job advert or job spec carefully; read between the lines.

Second-guessing questions

Second-guessing questions prior to an interview means that you have a secret weapon to boost your interview performance. Look again at Adverts 1 and 2, and think about what questions they will need to ask to check each applicant against their own obvious and subtext criteria. Try the Adverts Quiz below and see how you do. I have listed many potential and usual interview questions, but some would be definite questions and others less likely. See how many definites you score.

Adverts Quiz

Questions they may ask	Definite or Unlikely
1 What experience do you have of website maintenance/customer service?	
2 Give me an example of how you work well on your own.	
3 How would you deal with difficult people?	
4 What's important about communicating on the telephone?	
5 What sort of leadership skills do you have?	
6 When have you worked in a team to achieve a successful outcome?	
7 How do you plan your work?	
8 How serious are you in a working environment?	
9 How would you sell the benefits of our organisation without being pushy or aggressive?	
10 Do you like focusing on one thing at a time?	

Now all of these questions could be potential interview questions, but the most likely questions would be questions 1, 4, 6, 7 and 9.

▓ Question 1 is from the obvious requirements of Advert 1.

▓ Question 4 is suggested in both jobs, in particular through the customer-service aspect of Advert 2.

▓ Question 6 is a common question, but as both jobs mention teamwork, it is sure to come up.

▓ Question 7 is suggested in both adverts by words like 'ability to prioritise' and 'work to deadlines' – in fact they have virtually given you the answer they want to hear.

▓ Question 9 is relevant to Advert 2 – obviously a charity has to be promoted, and the challenge is to do this assertively but not aggressively.

Question 2 is unlikely to be asked because neither job seems to want an individualist who just likes to work alone. This might be a good quality for some jobs, but it does not seem to be required by these two adverts. Similarly, leadership skills do not seem to be required, so Question 5 would not be relevant.

Both adverts suggest a fun but hard-working environment, so I suspect they would not use the word 'serious' as in Question 8, unless they were hoping you would say,

'I'm not very serious in the sense that I like to enjoy myself in my work and ensure a happy environment, but I am quite serious in my approach to what needs to be done.'

Question 10 suggests someone who would have the luxury of specialising in a few key areas, and both jobs suggest a range of job duties all competing for attention and time, so this is another unlikely question.

Analysing the job description helps you know whether you are fit enough for their purposes, and knowing this can help you decide whether this is a job you want. Use both the obvious criteria and the subtext you guess at as a checklist to mark yourself against – if you match all or most of them, then this is a job for you.

Training regime Phase 2: Finding your USP

USP is an advertising term short for Unique Selling Point, but it is also a useful term for some unusual or special characteristic that each person has when applying for a job. It might be just the personal quality, skill or experience that you are proudest of. You might have boundless energy, speak fluent Urdu, or have met your MP through your hospital radio experience – these could all be USPs that an employer might be glad to know about.

Trawl through your life so far and try to pinpoint a time when you did something unusual or earned some commendation; or when you used some unusual skill. Here are some examples gathered from people I know –

Katie helped out with Meals on Wheels for two years. In itself this is fairly unique, but one time when she found an old lady unconscious, she had to call the ambulance and reassure the old lady. **USP: dealing with a crisis.**

Hafizah was on the events committee at college and took on the organising of a highly successful karaoke night. **USP: budgeting/leadership/PR.**

James saved someone's life in his job as a lifeguard. **USP – high-level rescue skills/calmness under pressure.**

Jonah ran a marathon for charity. **USP: physical fitness/determination.**

Miriam took six months off and travelled round Europe. She planned the whole trip and financed it herself by working beforehand and taking fruit-picking jobs where necessary. **USP: resourceful/determined.**

Jack decided he wanted a moped and saved his deposit in two months by taking on extra work. **USP: determination.**

Don't be put off if you don't seem to have USPs like these – just being friendly and approachable or being a natural sportsperson can be a USP. Think hard and ask friends and family and you will learn just how unique you are.

Training regime Phase 3: Research the employer

So many people don't bother to do this, but it is a fascinating and valuable way of knowing what to expect at the interview. If you have analysed the job description/spec/role, you will have gleaned some useful background information, but now you need to take it to the next level.

Some of the ways you could research the company are:

- The Internet – do a Google search (www.google.co.uk) or check if the company has a website. If it doesn't have a website, there may still be an article about it archived on the Internet, so it's worth checking. If the company does have a website, you will learn a lot about it, including the type of company it is and how it goes about its business.
- Companies House or business directories have in-depth information about many organisations – check at a good library.
- Ask people you know what they might know about a company or organisation.
- Phone the main switchboard and ask the receptionist if there is any marketing material that could be sent to you.
- If it is possible, make a sneaky research trip to the company premises and observe what people wear and what the offices are like. This can be useful as a way of getting a feel for the organisation or company culture that you might have to fit into.

Turning failure into feedback

Finally, we often fail to use the best piece of our experience to prepare for interviews – that is, when we forget to find out why we didn't succeed at a previous interview. There are so many variables in interviews that even with a great performance, you may miss being selected for the job. Someone else might have a 'desirable' they want or additional experience or qualifications. Sometimes there is a just a sliver of difference between one applicant and another. You might be beating yourself up mentally over something that had no bearing on why you were not picked. Finding out is called asking for feedback and most good employers will he happy to offer this.

If they phone you with their decision, you can use the opportunity to ask for feedback. You might say:

'Thank you for getting back to me in person. Of course, I'm disappointed, but I would appreciate some idea of how I could improve my interview performance for the next time. Could you give me some objective feedback?'

You can then use this information to improve your self-awareness for a future interview, or be comforted that there was nothing else you could have done.

Similarly, if you get written notification (a rejection letter), then phone and ask for feedback – it really is worth doing. Everything I know about my own interview performance has come from feedback I requested.

So that's what you need to know about pulling out your optimum performance, but if you still have some interview anxieties, Chapter 6 is designed to disperse these entirely.

6

Performance
anxiety

You don't need me to tell you that any kind of anxiety can cause counterproductive or sabotaging thoughts that will leak out in your performance at interview (see Chapter 4 for more on this). Nonetheless, for most people it is the fear of having to perform – of being judged and assessed – that causes the greatest interview stress.

To combat this interview stress, you need a greater understanding of how you are being assessed and what is being picked up. As mentioned previously, there have been many interesting studies on how we form impressions about other people and, of course, interviewers are doing just that – forming an impression of you. There are many examples of the amount of time it might take for someone to make a judgement, positive or negative, about someone else in a random encounter. As a general rule, scientists have found that we make up our mind about other people in a lightning and even illogical fashion.

Caveman stuff again

Our cave-dwelling ancestors had to make decisions fast in order to survive – they had to be able to notice a sabre-toothed tiger on the far horizon and judge by its body language whether it was hungry or just out for a walk. This is a survival mechanism we all possess, although some people have honed it more than others.

HERE'S HOW THIS SURVIVAL MECHANISM SEEMS TO WORK:

Each one of us is programmed to pick up signals from other people. We take in someone in a visual way, but this is in a far more in-depth way than just an analysis of what the person is wearing, the colour of their hair and so on. We are programmed to pick up clues about someone from their posture, their skin tone, the way their eyes move, even their breathing (which we can see by their chest movement). This information is taken in and processed at an incredible speed by our clever brains, and a first impression is formed.

As you know already, research suggests that this first impression is formed in anything from thirty seconds to four to five minutes – often referred to as the 'halo effect' – and this, for good or for bad, massively influences how we rate another person.

How these first impressions are transmitted

Most of the clues we pick up about other people are signs and signals that the person is barely aware of but are a strong indication of what they are really thinking about. Typically, if you watch someone on a bus or train, you can often tell by their face or posture how they are feeling – try this guessing game yourself sometime.

When you walk into an interview, everything you are thinking and feeling is written on your face and in your posture and body language for all to see. If you are thinking, 'This is going to be torture', your face might be a bit screwed up or your shoulders might be tense and a vaguely negative impression will be conveyed. If you are thinking, 'I'm going to show them that I am the right person for this job', it is likely that your posture will be relaxed and alert, and your face will show readiness for the challenge – all positive impressions.

Having the power and knowledge to control these first impressions is a key confidence-builder and a great defuser of performance anxiety, so take some time to learn all about this.

Some experts believe that a positive first impression can influence the interviewers to such a degree that if you get this right, you make it 75 per cent likely that you will be offered the job.

This may seem incredible, but it is worth stating that, even without opening your mouth or answering a single question, you might be able to convince interviewers that you are the perfect applicant.

Take control of your first-impression signals

The job is virtually yours if you can become an expert in your own body language and maximise the first few minutes of the interview impression. But how can you do this, I can hear you ask, when most of these messages you send are at an unconscious level?

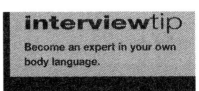

interviewtip

Become an expert in your own body language.

The mind/body connection

Sit in front of a full-length mirror, or at least just watch your face in a mirror. Think about a happy time. Really remember the detail of that time – close your eyes if it helps.

Now open your eyes and notice how your face looks, how your shoulders seem and any general impression you get. Write these details down.

Shake that good memory off and now start thinking of a time in your life when things went wrong or you failed an exam, or even of someone who really drives you crazy. Really get into it.

Now open your eyes again and notice how your face looks – the position of your shoulders, any impression you get. Write it down, then compare your notes.

Happy-thought body language

You will find that when you were thinking happy thoughts, there were certain signs to read. Here are some examples:

* Your facial muscles relax, your jaw drops slightly, your skin tone might be slightly warmer (caused by blood flow to the face).
* Your shoulders will possibly drop slightly and your breathing may deepen.

Bad-thought body language

When you think bad thoughts, mostly the opposite happens – your jaw might be tenser, your face may be tighter, your skin tone might be neutral, your shoulders will rise so they almost seem to touch your ears and your breathing may be high on your chest.

Now this is all quite subtle and mysterious stuff, but is powerful nonetheless in that it allows others to guess our fame of mind. So remember this – burn it on your memory –

THOUGHTS AND FEELINGS SHOW ON YOUR FACE AND IN YOUR PHYSIOLOGY.

Physiology workout

You need to have the power to banish negative thoughts and feelings. There are two easy ways to do this. I call them the inside–out workouts and outside–in workouts

Inside–out workout

As a general rule, our thoughts influence our feelings. If I think, 'Interviews are torture', my feelings are likely to be anxious and stressful. If it is true that whatever you think and feel on the inside leaks out onto the outside, then by choosing what you think you can control your physiology. I could choose to think, for example, 'Interviews are just a conversation,' or, 'I am interviewing them to see if I like them enough to work there.'

By doing this type of positive thinking as a preparation for the interview, I can work out mentally so that my physiology (face/shoulders/posture) gives off positive signals. This is often referred to by psychologists as 'cognitive rehearsal'. Cognition is just a word meaning the thoughts that we control and direct. You can control and direct your thoughts in this way by choice and, by doing that, influence the signals you send out.

Outside–in workout

As the mind–body link goes one way – that is, your mind affects your body language – so it can go the other way, too – your body can affect your mind. If your shoulders are tense because you have been thinking bad thoughts, you could try bouncing on a trampoline or hitting a squash ball and pretty soon that tenseness will have evaporated and any mind tenseness will have disappeared, too.

So, if you want to change a mental state, you can try some more **positive thinking** and do some physical activity to alter your body language. It's quite easy but powerful, and it's great that you can take some control over your own subconscious signals in this way.

Pre-interview tricks

1 If you travel in a car to an interview, sing loudly to your favourite CD – this is a voice warm-up and a good way of distracting you from negative thought (more about this in the 'Toning it up' section later).

2 Arrive early enough to take a walk around the block to stretch your muscles.

3 Nip into the toilets and do some stretches. Stand tall and stretch your arms above your head and then take ten good deep breaths with your eyes closed. Make sure that you breathe deep into your stomach and that your belly pushes out because you have filled your lungs and they are pushing at your stomach. This type of breathing will help your voice project better as well as relaxing you.

4 Have your mantras memorised – the things you want to say to yourself to calm your thoughts and programme yourself positively. Try 'I know I am right for this job,' 'I can show them what I can offer,' 'I am so excited by the chances offered in this job role,' or even, 'This will go well and they are sure to want me.'

5 While waiting to go in, stay centred, remembering to keep the deep breathing going, though without panting loudly of course! This is the time to run your own cognitive-rehearsal thought loop (see below).

6 Finally, remember that **projection is perception**, which means what you project is what is you are perceiving at that moment in time; that is, those distracting thoughts that your mind gets sucked into. And what you project is then perceived and noted by the interviewer. So any way that you can practise controlling what you project will be of great value. Here are two techniques that can really help with this:

Monitor your thoughts

Be a thought policeman for a few days. When we are going about our lives, random thoughts come and go and are often quite harmless. Nonetheless, in certain situations we have a tendency to dive into a downward-spiral thought loop which is more damaging. If I am a little nervy about parking in busy cities, I might be thinking,

'I'll probably never find a car-park space; the car parks will be full, and I'll end up driving round around in a strange one-way system all the time with cars honking at me.'

This thought loop will mean that my brain inadvertently ends up focusing on what I am thinking of – that is, I will be thinking of *not* finding a car-park space. If I chose some different thought patterns such as,

'There will be some spaces if I keep my eyes open for signs and if I keep my wits about me,'

then it is more likely that I will notice car-park signs because – here is the amazing thing – by thinking positively, I instruct my brain to do what I need it to do. In this case, I am saying, 'Find a car park!'

So here's what you need to try. Over a few days, notice the quality of your thoughts, vet them for their value to you. If you are constantly overwhelmed by negative thoughts, you are just shooting yourself in the foot. Every time you notice a negative thought, restate it mentally in the positive. Practise switching your thinking onto more useful thought tracks, then you will be ready to try our second technique – cognitive rehearsal.

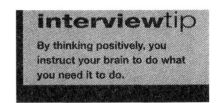

interviewtip

By thinking positively, you instruct your brain to do what you need it to do.

Cognitive rehearsal – a proven way to prepare for interviews

Without realising it, most people prepare for interviews by imagining negative scenarios. They run these thought loops over and over as they get nearer the interview date – they do a very good job of programming themselves to fail. These catastrophic scenarios sabotage their chances of being resourceful in interview situations.

Cognitive rehearsal is a natural thing we all do – we imagine how things will go mentally, based on previous experiences or what we have heard from others. However, **we do have a choice about how we think** – if we imagine ourselves performing and projecting brilliantly, seeing and hearing how it will go in the most optimistic scenario, we are more likely to mirror or recreate that in the actual interview.

If you imagine a catastrophic scenario often enough, your mind thinks that that is what you want and does its best to make that happen by sending out confusing signals, which result in another bad experience to use in your negative cognitive rehearsals in the future.

Successful athletes use cognitive rehearsal to rev up for a race or event – they see themselves breaking through the tape ahead of the field, hearing the roar of the crowd, and feel the feeling of running fluidly. They don't see themselves coming last! If you want to almost immunise yourself against needless performance anxiety, cognitive rehearsal of the positive kind is just what you need. Here's how to do it.

Ideally you should do this about two weeks before the interview. Take a quiet moment when you can go into this relaxation and visualisation technique.

Positive cognitive rehearsal: stage one

Relax in a chair or lying down – mentally work through your body from your feet to your head, tensing and then relaxing muscles until you feel like you are sinking down or are like a rag doll, completely floppy.

Focus on your breathing – mentally track the in and out breaths – then after a while begin to focus on the breath coming in through your nose and keeping your mouth shut, then allow the breath to come out of your nose in a natural way. Begin to breathe in through the nose, counting to five mentally, and then breathe out to a count of five.

After a few minutes of this, let your breathing slip into its natural rhythm.

Now, remember a time of great achievement or success – or just a time when you felt really good or had a sense of doing well. Take a moment and remember that time. As you remember that time you may find that you see what you saw that day – if you have any memories like that, enjoy them, picturing how it was in any way you can.

Then, as you remember that time, it may be that you hear voices or sounds from that time or even the voice in your head. If you do, hear what you heard that day – let yourself enjoy that remembering.

Then, as you remember that time, it may be that you remember the feeling you felt that day. Let yourself remember, and feel what you felt.

Now whatever you remembered, hold those thoughts and memories and enjoy them.

This is your calming resource state – a state you can return to every day until your interview by just going through that sequence – it takes ten minutes at most. This is the first phase of your cognitive rehearsal and can be done on its own any time you need to feel pumped up and resourceful. Practising it regularly will mean that you can call up the memory in an instant to calm yourself in any stressful situation.

You can do a short-cut version, standing in a bus queue without doing the relaxation and breathing part (this might cause stares or whispers!) Of course, this short-cut version will become a new thought programme that you can use in any stressful situation, but especially just before you go into an interview. This alone will ensure that the look on your face and your posture and body language are relaxed when you walk into the interview and will ensure a powerful first impression.

Now the next stage is to practise the actual cognitive rehearsal of how you want the interview to be – the 'as if' or rehearsal state. This can follow on from your resource state and can be done each day before your interview to rev yourself up mentally. Doing the two together is the perfect antidote to interview nerves.

Positive cognitive rehearsal: stage two

Following on from your resource state, take a moment to think of how you would like the interview to go in great detail, from beginning to end.

You may be able to see yourself walking in confidently and/or see yourself taking a seat and smiling and greeting people. You may see yourself in the room, facing your interviewers, looking good and ready and alert. **See how it will be.**

It may be that you can hear yourself dealing with all the questions, handling them well, giving just the right answers, really listening to their questions, responding perfectly. **Hear how it will be.**

It may be that you have an excited feeling at the beginning, and you begin to feel more and more confident as you feel them liking you and feel that they think you are doing well. Or it may be just that you feel good and on top form. **Feel how it will be.**

Hold the memory you have created – a memory of how it could be, how you would like it to be and enjoy it.

After a little time, bring yourself back to awareness of your surroundings.

Practise this over and over so that it becomes as real as a normal memory and easy to access at any time. Use this prior to interview to programme your thoughts and increase your confidence – it really works. You can use the words 'remember that time' to access the resource state and 'see/hear/feel how it will be' to access your 'as if' or rehearsal state.

Most people who appear confident perform naturally in an 'as if' state when they are doing something new or unfamiliar. This means that instinctively they start to imagine what they would be like if they were 100 per cent confident. For example, you have to do a presentation and you are somewhat nervous. Imagine yourself doing this confidently – what would you look like, sound like, feel like? How would you stand? Would you move around? How loud would your voice be? The 'as if' state gives you lots of new information to include in a new thought programme that will help you 'act confidently'.

Other rehearsal techniques

There are some other simple ways that you can get some practice and valuable feedback for interviews. Here are a few ideas to try –

- Get a friend to ask you some typical interview questions – use the list in Chapter 8. First aim for fluent answers by preparing in your mind how you would answer each question. Then try again, running through the questions and asking for feedback on your fluency or responses to questions. Run it all again. This time, ask your friend to give you feedback on your body language. Try again as many times as you need until it begins to feel very natural (you will owe this friend big time!).
- You can do something similar with a tape recorder or Dictaphone in place of a friend. Record the questions onto a tape, leaving spaces for your answers, then run the tape with you answering the questions. Play the tape back and analyse how well you have done, without being unnecessarily critical. Try it again and again until it improves.
- A friend with a video recorder or camera could help in just the same way so that you can gain valuable feedback.
- Interview coaching by a careers adviser or even a family friend or relative (who may work in a personnel department) is also very useful. Check out what is available.

Finally, back to thought monitoring. There is some reason to believe that the language you use about an interview can influence your feelings of anxiety, so you might want to ban words like 'torture', 'minefield', 'interrogation', and even 'nervous' and 'scared' from your vocabulary, as they may induce a negative state. Keep your words neutral regarding the interview and save your passion and emotion to fuel your enthusiasm in the actual interview situation.

7

Real-world interview scenarios – What they will throw at you

Let's demystify interviews further by considering exactly what types and styles of interview you might be likely to come across. In this way, they will all become so familiar that you can face whatever you encounter with a calm confidence.

Recruiters generally choose their interview format and approach according to a number of key factors, which are –

- what they want to find out about you
- the equal-opportunities policy of the organisation
- the kind of job role
- how much they've already guessed about you as a result of your CV or application form.

Picking the wrong person as a result of an interview process is every employer's nightmare, so good employers do everything they can to ensure that the interview really produces the information they need to make the best decision. It costs them money and time if they pick the wrong person. So it stands to reason that, given that for most employers recruitment interviews take their time away from other things, they need to plan the process and conduct interviews in a professional way.

The professional way to set up interviews

This is the likely process they will go through –

1 They analyse what it is they want the job holder to do – they create a job spec (sometimes called the 'person spec') or job description or sometimes a job role profile (see more about definitions of these words in 'Talking in code' in Chapter 8)

2 They advertise and receive applications which they longlist and/or shortlist (we talked about this in Chapter 3). If they are doing this properly, they will do it in an almost scientific and objective way; that means they will compare their spec with each applicant's declared information and pick out only those that meet their requirements most perfectly.

3 They decide on an interview format (see below), which will be most likely to generate information from the applicant that helps them make a good decision.

4 Letters are sent out inviting applicants to interviews.

5 All interviewers will be briefed together so that a common approach is decided. The purpose of the interviews is clearly explained and suitable interview questions are identified and shared out.

6 Decisions will be made as to how and when to inform applicants of their success or failure and whether feedback will be offered.

What they want to find out about you

This is somewhat simple and complex at the same time. In simple terms they want to find out whether you match their requirements from the job spec.

In more complex terms there are all kinds of deeper concerns they may have which are –

- whether the 'you' presented in your CV/application form, and even at interview, is an accurate representation of what you will be like in the work role
- whether nervousness might obscure the real 'you' and how to overcome this
- whether your personality will fit that company or the team you have to work for
- whether you can develop further and become an amazingly useful employee
- whether you can help them be more profitable and/or more successful.

The best way to try and understand this is by imagining that you are planning a holiday; your idea of the kind of holiday you want is pretty much like the job description an employer creates – you have some essential and desirable criteria just like they do. You might want:

- a beach
- nightlife
- self-catering apartment

- Greece
- a cheap deal.

Now when you look in the brochure or talk to a travel agent you are in fact running an interview process to check what will be best for you from various equally appealing holidays. This checking process is important because you don't want to end up in the wrong place in a resort that really doesn't fit your expectations. You will ask the travel agent questions that will help you determine exactly what the different holiday possibilities offer – the brochure version may sound and look good, but you will want to check that **what seems good is in fact what it claims to be.**

In the same way, in the interview they are checking out whether the brochure version of 'you' reflects a real, living, breathing person that they can imagine working for them and that your 'you' is a little bit, or even a lot, better than someone else whom they interview.

The company's equal-opportunities policy

As you probably know, it is illegal to discriminate against someone on grounds of race, culture, gender, sexual orientation or disability in the interview process, and so employers generally make great efforts to assess each applicant objectively and in a standard way to avoid negatively discriminatory practice.

This means that they will probably create a standard list of questions, which they will ask of each applicant. They will set up the interview in a format that someone else could scrutinise and deem to be fair to everyone. They will use a scoring system to score you against all the essential and desirable criteria, and whichever applicant achieves the highest score of ticks against their requirements will be offered the job.

Whatever you might have heard about interviewers, it is not in their interests to do any of the following:

- Sit you on a small chair to make you feel ill at ease
- Place you in a chair with sun blazing into your face
- Ask trick questions
- Set up scary scenarios to test your ability to withstand pressure.

Experienced interviewers know that these tactics could open them up to accusations of unfairness, or even illegal practice, and that they would, in any case, be counterproductive because they would not help them make good recruitment decisions.

Making things as equal and fair to all applicants is a proven method of professional recruitment, and you will find that most organisations will try their best to conduct interviews in a professional way. Nonetheless, the kind of job role can determine the process of questioning and their approach, but this still ought to be framed in an equal-opportunities way.

The kind of job role

If you went for a job as a counsellor, the questions asked would be about your professional ethic and the way you work, but given that counsellors are meant to listen more than talk, they will be judging you on your listening powers as you go through the interview. If you go for a legal job, which may require negotiating skills and the ability to communicate assertively, they will expect to find these qualities in the way you respond to questions.

The way you perform at interview is taken as a reflection of how you might perform in the job, so if, for example, you come across as very quietly spoken and nervy, you might not score highly for a job as a call-centre operator.

How much they've guessed about you from your CV/application form

Employers don't want to rely on guesswork, which is why they want to interview you – they want to check out the reality and confirm their opinion of you. This is why it is foolish to make grand or unsubstantiated claims in your application (remember that e word – evidence). Don't describe yourself as outgoing and confident if you know you will not be able to create that impression at interview – you might call yourself 'quietly confident' instead.

interviewtip

Don't make grand or unsubstantiated claims in your application – the most important thing is to come across as a genuine and authentic person.

The most important thing is to come across as a genuine and authentic person. If they don't want you in your truly authentic way, then you don't fit their requirements – you won't like the job, you won't like working there and

YOU SHOULD THANK THEM FOR NOT PICKING YOU!

Now let's get into how interviews might map out so that you know what to expect.

The professional (and usual) way to interview applicants

Here are some key general interview patterns. Some or all of these might occur at your interview.

- Many interviews are conducted by a panel of interviewers, often made up of three people – perhaps a member of personnel, the manager of the department and one other. Some interviews are conducted by just one or two people.
- Interviewers often sit behind a desk or table with paper to take notes and with copies of your application form or CV in their hands.
- You will be asked to sit, often opposite them, although they may have attempted to make the setting more informal, say, with you all sitting round a round table.
- The chair of the interview panel (the leader of the pack, so to speak) may sit in the middle and may be the first to greet you and introduce the other panel members.
- This person might explain the format of the interview, something like 'We aim to find out how you fit our requirements and we want you to feel free to ask questions at any time. We will not be asking you any trick questions. We want you to give us the chance to get to know you and what you can offer us. We plan to ask eight specific questions, which we will take it in turn to ask you. At the end, we will be happy to answer any further questions you might have for us. Does that seem OK for you?'
- The interview will start and run its course. Finally you are given the chance to ask your questions. You will be told when you might expect to hear their decision, and they will thank you for attending.

There may be variations on this format, but, broadly speaking, that is the way it will probably go.

The way to manage panel interviews

The main challenge here is who to look at, as there are a few people you might possibly focus on. Have a look at the plan below.

Who do you look at?

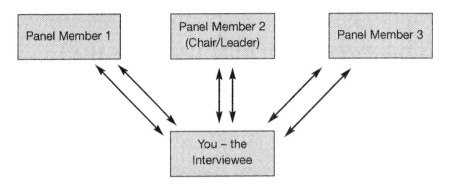

You have three pairs of eyes to make contact with, and that's pretty difficult to do, so here's what you can do:

- Sit straight in your chair, pulling the bottom of your spine to the furthest back point of the chair seat, using the chair back to support you lightly.
- Move your head and brush the panel with your eyes, starting at the left of you and moving across to the right. Then straighten up and focus on the chair/leader who is likely to start talking first.
- Focus on the person who is speaking and, keeping your torso straight and centred, turn your head to the person who is asking the question.
- Answer the question with your face still turned towards the questioner's face, giving them gentle eye contact.
- Having finished answering, brush the other members of the panel with your eyes and centre yourself again for the next question.

This is like a rhythmic dance, with you just moving your head to show interest and managing the situation in the best way. By doing this, you engage the whole panel and maintain rapport with all of them throughout the process.

interviewtip

Engage the whole panel and maintain rapport with them throughout the interview.

This also helps with any feelings you might have due to the fact that there are more of them than there are of you – it can sometimes feel as if you're being ganged up on! By dealing with them individually and pulling them in in this way, you can defuse the confrontational feel of a panel interview and put yourself back in control.

One-to-one interviews

There are various reasons for a one-to-one interview. It may be that the company is small, and your interview is not with some personnel or human-resource (HR) person but with the owner or managing director. It may be company policy to offer a first interview on a one-to-one basis – just you and a manager, say – and then follow this up with a second interview, which might be a panel interview. Conversely, you may get through a panel interview first and then be offered a second-stage one-to-one interview.

Here are some characteristics of one-to-one interviews:

- They may seem less formal.
- They may seem quite intimate, almost conversational.
- They may seem either less threatening or more threatening.

The **informality** can be good if it relaxes you a little and allows you to be yourself. It can be bad if you take the process less seriously. It's a careful balance. The person is still assessing you, so don't allow the informality to make you lose track of what it's all about.

The **intimacy** might again tempt you to relax, but remember again that if this means you lose your alertness, a question might trip you up.

The **more threatening/less threatening** conundrum will depend on you. If you feel stressed by a panel, you might find this easier; but it could slip into interrogation-mode territory too, so just be aware of your own feelings and respond from your strong resourceful place at all times (remember 'cognitive rehearsal' in Chapter 6).

EXAMPLES OF PANEL AND ONE-TO-ONE INTERVIEWS

Here's an example of the panel interview in its most positive light –

Lucas

Lucas walked into the interview to find a spacious, well-lit room. He was offered a drink of water and was offered a seat at a round table alongside the two interviewers. He had prepared a presentation on a laptop computer (see Chapter 10), which he set up next to him with the small screen facing both interviewers. This is how it looked:

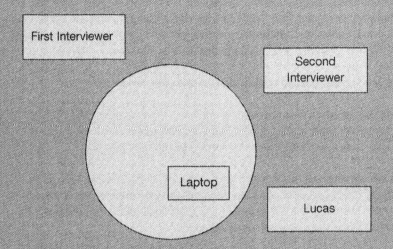

This was a comforting and unthreatening set-up for the interview – Lucas felt like an equal sitting round the table – and the initial questions they asked him felt like a **conversation with a purpose**. He was relaxed and alert at the same time.

In the second part of the interview, Lucas talked through his presentation while sitting down, which felt quite natural and yet very professional. On the basis of this performance, Lucas was offered a second interview (see below).

Here's a similarly positive example of a one-to-one interview that Vickram experienced when he applied for a part-time job in a university library –

Vickram

Vickram applied for the part-time library job because it would fit around his studies and offered flexible hours. The letter inviting to interview actually offered him the chance of an informal chat with the senior librarian and a look round the library and learning resource. This was an optional interview or informal chat, which would take place a week before his main interview. This is quite a common practice and is an ideal preparation for the main interview.

When he arrived, he was taken on a tour of the library and then they sat down in a small office where the senior librarian talked through the job description. Vickram had the chance to talk about his course, his use of the library as a student and ask questions about library routines and hours of work. Their conversation was chatty but again with a clear purpose on both sides – the senior librarian offered an interesting insight into the behind-the-scenes work of the library. Vickram was able to impress the senior librarian by his quiet confidence and serious attitude. At the main interview, Vickram felt calm and centred and was offered the job.

Second interviews

It's not always clear whether an organisation will hold first and second interviews. Sometimes it can be a bit frustrating to be offered a second interview. One student went through a quite high-powered interview for an accountancy placement, only to find that there was more to come. This is how he saw it –

'I prepared myself for one high-pressure interview, did my research, practised questions and thought that the interview went brilliantly. It couldn't have gone better! And then they tell me that I need to wait to hear whether I've made it into the second-interview batch! It drove me crazy! I'm not sure I can go through it all again.'

Going through it all again

Here's the good and bad news – bad news first.

Competition for certain jobs means bucket loads of applicants. Rather than shortlist down to only a few candidates, some employers want to give more applicants a chance so they offer a first-shortlisting type of interview. In many ways this is quite fair and should be commended.

A first interview can be a more 'getting to know you' interview and often means that a more nervous applicant can gain confidence for the next stage. If a recruiter is uncertain about someone's paper application, it gives her the chance to check someone out, especially if he or she is a non-standard applicant. Take a look at the following case study:

case study

Jenny

Jenny had missed out on college because she became a young single parent at 16. On paper she didn't have any qualifications, but her voluntary experience with a charity doing fundraising suggested she could be persuasive and determined, both useful qualities for the job she applied for in customer service for a mail-order catalogue. A first interview gave her the chance to shine and helped her get into the second-interview sift.

The good news if you get a second interview is:

- They liked you and want to get to know you better.
- You made an impression, and they will remember you.
- You feel more comfortable with them and know something about the company/organisation.
- The odds of you being offered the job have drastically improved.

First interviews are a way of screening applicants – a way for recruiters to sift out the not-so-suitable from the suitable. Other common screening methods are telephone interviews and email interviews.

Telephone interviews

These can be used as a timesaver for recruiters or a very appropriate way of testing out applicants.

With popular jobs, you may be asked to phone for an application pack – even the message you leave on the answer phone may be scrutinised for qualities they require. So be aware and follow the telephone guidelines offered below. In other situations, the job advert might ask you to phone for an informal chat or interview with a specified person.

Do not take this as a sign that you can avoid being assessed and measured – it may seem natural or informal, but nonetheless their questions will be framed with a clear purpose – can you fulfil their requirements? Sometimes these sifting-type interviews can last only minutes so the pressure is on to send out the right signals and offer crisp and evidence-based answers – that is, you have to prove to them that you can do the job by giving them examples of your suitability.

In other cases, telephone interviews are used because the nature of the job as advertised requires telephone skills and so a telephone interview is one of the best ways of measuring this skill. Here is a sample of a real telephone interview Ella had for a telephone customer-service role with a bank.

Ella	Hello, my name is Ella Mirella. Can I speak to Jane Gardner please? I'm ringing to apply for the role of telephone customer-service assistant.
Jane	Hello, Ella, I'm Jane Gardner. Thank you for calling. We're telephone interviewing a number of applicants. Can I start by asking you some questions about your experience?
Ella	That's fine, Jane. My main customer-service experience has been through my retail work in the Biggles Department Store. Obviously this is face-to-face customer service – advising customers, dealing with credits and refunds and processing stock enquiries. However, I do have responsibility for ordering specialist items for customers, and this involves telephone work with buyers, suppliers and, eventually, the customers to inform them of delivery dates.
Jane	Thank you – that's useful to know. Ella, what would you say is the most important thing about communicating on the telephone?
Ella	Well, I always try and think what I want to say before I pick up the phone ... and I try and speak clearly. I suppose it's important also to listen to exactly what is being said so that I can make sure I have all the details. I also try to be very polite and introduce myself properly, staying pleasant even when people are less than polite themselves.
Jane	Thank you, Ella. That's enough for today. You've just got yourself through to a second-stage interview. Well done! I'll be in touch by letter.

And that's how it went. You'll find that telephone interviews are often quite short but they work quite well in finding out who has and hasn't got a good telephone manner. Jane Gardner was able to analyse what Ella said and most importantly how she said it.

How to be great on the telephone

- Be prepared – some people prepare a short introductory script. For example – 'Hello, I'm Jamie Jamieson, and I'm ringing about ...'.
- Be prepared – analyse the job description – what will they want to know about you?
- Sing loudly before the phone call to loosen up your voice.
- Take about ten good deep breaths.
- Stand up while on the phone, relax your shoulders and your voice will project better.

- Make sure you are somewhere private and will not be interrupted.
- Preferably use a main-line phone rather than your mobile – the connection is likely to be better. If you do use your mobile, make sure you have enough credit and the connection is good.
- Introduce yourself clearly and ask for the named person in the advert.
- Be courteous but not fawning – thank them at the end.

Email screening

You may be screened on the telephone or via email – here's how to deal with the email challenge. This is principally an electronic version of the phone interview, which can either be run 'real time' or through a sequence of questions in one email or a sequence of emails.

'Real time' would mean an invitation to a specific interview chat room or discussion forum at a specific time when someone will type questions which you will then type answers to. In this scenario, give yourself time to think and again do your homework beforehand by analysing what they might want. Sign in clearly with your name and sign off with your personal contact details (phone and email).

Alternatively, you might be emailed a series of questions, which you then have to respond to. As a result of your answers, supplementary questions might also be emailed to you.

The same rules apply here as on application forms – they can't see or hear you, so everything you write has to hit their selection buttons, so be sure to research them well to ensure you make the second sift.

And finally, whatever interview format you encounter, the preparation work you've done on yourself and in researching the employer will act as armour against mishaps. Let's move on now to the aspect of interviews that causes the most confusion and stress – the actual questions that will be asked.

8

The answer is in
the question

Everyone who goes for interview obsesses about the questions they might be asked, when in fact they can often deal with the most important bit by getting the first impression right as discussed in Chapter 4. Frequently, applicants find that if have prepared thoroughly and are in the optimum resourceful state (see Chapter 6), they can sense the best interview answers from the phrasing of the question. To do this, you need to be in a mental state of readiness, so that you really, really listen to the questions.

Nonetheless, the questions they ask can cause some concern, so let's start by analysing the types of question you might be asked and the 'code' language used by interviewers that can sometimes confuse us.

Common questions

There are three questions that occur the most frequently at interviews, so much so that they are almost boring. Can you guess which they are from the list below?

What qualifications do you have that most suit this job?
Where do you see yourself five years from now?
What are your strengths and weaknesses?
Why did you apply for this job?
What do you think are your best skills?
What experience do you have of this kind of work?
What do you have to offer us?
What is your career plan?
Tell me about yourself.
How would your describe yourself?

While most of these questions are common to interviews and some are just variations on a theme, the three most frequently used questions are:

Why did you apply for this job?

This is essentially a question about your motivation to work for that employer and in that role, so show them that you match what they want and that you want truthfully and genuinely to work for them. Here's a sample answer:

'I like the idea of working for a large food company, and I enjoy the role of quality tester. I'm ready to take more responsibility. Moreover, I have always wanted to work for Foody Foods and know that I can operate well in the job role as senior quality tester.'

Tell me about yourself

There's an easy formula to follow for this one. This is an icebreaker question at the beginning of the interview but is an important scene setter.

Follow this sequence:

1 Currently I am … (what you are doing now)

2 Previously I … (what you did in the past that might seem relevant)

3 I am …(a brief description of yourself on top form)

An example of this might be:

'Currently I am working as an administrative assistant in an insurance company where I am responsible for support to insurance salesmen, including organising their appointments and keeping track of their paperwork.

Prior to this, I took a business and secretarial course at college, gaining my OCR qualifications and undertaking a work placement on a local newspaper.

I am self-motivated and organised and would love to work in advertising sales for your newspaper.'

This formula is easy to remember and effective – it gives just enough information as long as you remember to promote your best points.

What do you have to offer us?

This is a somewhat sly question as in some ways it really means 'Tell us why we should pick you.' Nonetheless, answering the surface question and the beneath-the-surface subtext is the best way to handle it. Here's a sample answer:

'You seem to be looking for someone with good organisational skills, an experience of electronics and accuracy and attention to detail. Well, I can prove to you that I am that kind of person through my previous experience. Over and above this, I would offer you hard work and enthusiasm and proven ability to stay calm in a crisis from my experience in the armed forces.'

Basically what you have to do is first explain how you perfectly match their criteria and then ideally give them your added value – the something extra, the USP (see Chapter 5), that will put you ahead of the other applicants. If they have suggested something desirable that they want and you know you have that something, then you might offer that as the added value.

Three-point answers

If you're wondering when to stop talking when you start answering an interview question, it's worth focusing on the three- or four-point rule. Most of us cannot retain more than three or four points at a time, so offer the interviewer three or four clear points (about three or four sentences' worth) and then stop! Make sure you have an idea of three or four points you plan to make for each potential question.

Get a friend to practise asking you the common questions, and you can practise giving them your three-point answers. Of course, while you might learn these answers in this artificial way, you will need to deliver them with feeling.

Now, as mentioned before, most of the other questions are just variations of those three and by using your self-audit from Chapter 2 and completing the grid below, you will have all you need to answer these questions.

Interview questions 'miracle grid'		
	What you've got	**For example (evidence)**
Personality qualities – pick three strengths		
Three best skills or abilities		
Interests/hobbies that might suggest good things about you		
Experience		

Here's one completed for Sam:

Sam's interview preparation 'miracle grid'		
	What you've got	**For example (evidence)**
Personality qualities – pick three strengths	Confident, outgoing, motivated, competitive	Rugby captain, made speeches, bar work, hospitality and catering at events
Three best skills or abilities	Communication skills, leadership skills, well organised	Rugby captain, student-newspaper volunteer
Interests/hobbies that might suggest good things about you	Travel/reading thrillers	Gap year in Australia – working on fruit farms
Experience	Worked in insurance to earn money for gap year	Had to work to targets each month and deal with customers over phone

If you really can work out your best qualities, skills and experience, and offer some good examples to prove them, then you will be able to deal with most common interview questions. Interestingly, if you answer the first question they ask well, they occasionally barely have to ask you anything else.

Competency-based interviews

Public-service organisations such as the Civil Service use a competency-based framework for interviews, which means they use the job role to determine what competency the ideal applicant would need and then ask questions according to what would be needed to do the job. If the job role requires three or four main competencies, such as planning skills, knowledge of Microsoft Access, administrative experience and teamwork, the questions will focus specifically on these areas. They may also ask **situational questions** to determine someone's typical approach in a given situation.

Here are some examples of situational questions that aim to suggest real-world scenarios:

'Your team leader is sick and you have an irate client on the phone. What would you do?'

'A customer is on the phone and the file has gone missing. What would you do?'

'A colleague is not pulling his weight and the workload is suffering. What would you do?'

The point is with these questions that there is no real or perfect answer. They just want to test your thinking powers and ability to analyse and make a decision. The best approach is to follow this formula:

- Check what data/info you have about the situation (restate the basic details of the question).
- Consider all options and explain what seem to be the possibilities of approach or potential solutions.
- Pick one approach, which seems to be the most appropriate and justify it (explain your thinking and your judgement).

Hypothetical questions

These are very similar to situational questions but are phrased in a different way. They may seem a bit wild and wacky. They might ask, 'If you were stranded on a desert island with a group of people, what role would you take?' or, 'How would you react if someone told you they had committed a crime?'

Use the same approach as for situational questions – show your thinking and weighing up, make a decision, then justify it.

Subtext behind most questions – what on earth are they after?

They want to know something magic about you and you have to let that shine through. They want to get beneath your skin and know what makes you tick. They want to make the right choice from their shortlisted applicants.

Do you have any questions?

This can be the most important question at an interview, so don't miss the chance of showing interest by having a possible question ready. You could ask any of the following:

What kind of additional training might you want me to undertake?
How does the salary structure work?
How do you see the role developing?
When will I hear your decision? When can I expect to hear your decision?

Try not to ask a question that they have covered elsewhere, and if you simply have no questions, then answer 'No thank you. You've covered everything.'

Code language or interview and application jargon

If it seems as if the interviewers are talking in code or jargon, here is a list of the common terms and their meanings.

Word	Code meaning
Criteria	The exact skills and experience that they are looking for from the perfect applicant
Desirable	Something extra that they would like from applicants which would make a good applicant the ideal applicant
Engage/Rapport	This can mean anything you do in the interview, which helps you make a connection with the interviewer – it doesn't mean kissing or hugging them! It means how you show you are interested, the non-verbal signs that help them feel they know you in some way.
Essential	If this is listed in a job advert or job specification, it means that you should apply only if you possess the essential requirements that are listed.

Objective	Recruiters try to be objective when interviewing applicants, and this means that they match applicants against the strict requirements of the job role.
Person specification	This is what the employer thinks will be the ideal applicant – their list of personality qualities, skills, qualifications and experience that they consider are required for the job.
Shortlist	They have to pick a batch of people to interview from a large pool – the shortlist is made up of those applicants who seem to be most suitable.
Sift	Imagine you have to sift some flour through a sieve so that all the lumps are saved in the sieve and there is a pile of beautiful flour – employers sift through applications or CVs and decide which are lumpy and which are smooth. Smooth applicants are the ones that make an interview shortlist.
Terms and conditions	When an applicant is made a job offer after interview, the terms and conditions of the work are detailed in the letter, which confirms the job offer. These will include the hours of work, holiday entitlement, etc. – by agreeing to these terms and conditions you enter a contract with the employer and accept the job.

Simply the best advice and preparation tips

Don't go off into interview territory without a map – that is, an idea of the questions they will need to ask you to check you are the one.

Get in training by researching the employer and the job.

Mentally prepare yourself for what will be required – use cognitive rehearsal (see Chapter 6).

Try and think of an interview as a fact-finding mission – your research produces some of the facts, but the interview is your chance to take this further by interviewing them.

If a question seems a little mystifying, ask for it to be repeated in this way: 'I want to be clear what you are asking – could you just repeat the question?'

If asked a completely mystifying question such as 'Can you do differential calculus?' (and you know that you can't), try saying, 'I don't know anything about that, but I'm a quick learner and am willing to learn.'

And finally, think of yourself as a resourceful person who can deal with anything that gets thrown at you because you have taken the time to prepare and practise – you are like a well-trained athlete just raring to go and run the race!

9

What if they
offer you the
job, and what if
they don't?

Most interviews result in one of two possibilities – a yes or a no. Yes – they love you and you're just what they want; or no – you just don't match their spec. If it's yes, you did what you needed to do and persuaded them of your suitability. If it's no – there are a range of possible reasons why you weren't chosen:

1 You were so nervous you didn't make a strong case.

2 You got to the interview and found it wasn't what you thought and so, without realising, sent out 'Don't pick me' signals

3 You were just going for the job without any real passion for it and that came through.

4 You were having a bad day, a personal crisis; your head wasn't in the right place.

5 You have a mindset about being bad at interviews and you decided to prove it to yourself.

Possible reason Number 1

All you can do is learn from this by thinking through how you approached the interview and certainly by practising some of the mental-cognitive techniques in Chapter 6. Be brave and phone up and ask for feedback on your performance – it may be that you were better than you thought, but they appointed someone who could speak Swahili and you couldn't. Finally tell yourself the following –

'I didn't get it because there is something better around the corner.'

Ask anyone about the jobs they didn't get, and you'll find they are generally glad about it in retrospect.

Possible reason Number 2

You had a lucky break, so chalk it up to experience. But remember that your subconscious sent out signals that were picked up accurately – they read you well.

Possible reason Number 3

Don't go for a job that you don't want – it always leaks out and is a waste of time for you and them.

Possible reason Number 4

Bad things happen, but don't let them wind you up – there's always another interview.

Possible reason Number 5

A warped mindset is just a way of setting yourself up to fail – change the mindset! Phone and ask for feedback – it's quite likely that you did some things right, so build on those and change some of the ineffective things you did.

interviewtip

If you don't get a job, be brave and ask for feedback.

The job offer

Play the following job offer quiz game and decide what is the smart and less smart approach out of the following statements.

Job offer quiz		
Possible responses to job offer	Smart	Less smart
That's great – when can I start?		
I need to check with my current employer about my notice period. What else do you need to know from me?		

Possible responses to job offer	Smart	Less smart
I want that in writing before I give my answer.		
Thank you for the offer – I'm absolutely thrilled. What will happen next?		
What are the terms and conditions?		
Can you talk me through the offer, or will I receive something in writing in the next day or two?		
Do you mind my asking what salary I will get?		
I'm so surprised – I can't believe you picked me!		
I am really flattered to be offered this job. I'd like to take 24 hours to think about it fully – it would help if you could give me further details of the contract, the salary, etc.		

It may seem pretty obvious to you when you see the statements above which are the smarter responses, but often when an offer of job is made we are a little unprepared and come out with something which sounds awkward, demanding or downright humble.

The awkward, demanding or humble responses

What are the terms and conditions?

This is a little awkward and abrupt and could be softened by something like:

'Thank you for the offer. I'm really pleased. I'd be interested in hearing the exact terms and conditions of the contract. Can you talk me through them?'

I want that in writing before I give my answer.

This sounds aggressive and suggests a lack of trust in the employer – not a good way to start the relationship. It's quite smart to want to see the offer in writing but there are other ways to suggest this:

'Assuming your written offer matches what we've discussed, I will be thrilled to accept it,' or

'Thank you for the offer, which I look forward to receiving in writing. I'm looking forward to working for you.'

The 'thank you for the offer' and 'I'm looking forward' bits soften the 'in writing' request.

That's great – when can I start?

I'm so surprised – I can't believe you picked me!

Do you mind my asking what salary I will get?

All of these are a little humble and unassuming – you deserve this job offer so you don't need to be apologetic about it. The 'That's great – when can I start?' is not too bad, but that eagerness could be misinterpreted as desperation unless they have already given you the full details of the job offer and you know it is perfect.

The smart responses

'I need to check with my current employer about my notice period. What else do you need to know from me?'

'Thank you for the offer – I'm absolutely thrilled. What will happen next?'

'Can you talk me through the offer, or will I receive something in writing in the next day or two?'

'I am really flattered to be offered this job. I'd like to take 24 hours to think about it fully – it would help if you could give me further details of the contract, the salary, etc.'

These are smart responses because they come across as enthusiastic and professional.

If you expect to be offered the job as a result of a good interview performance, then you need to plan your response to the job offer, so that you don't feel awkward and blurt something out.

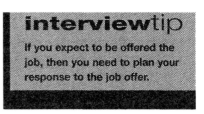

interviewtip

If you expect to be offered the job, then you need to plan your response to the job offer.

Negotiations

Again this can be done with assertiveness and tact rather than in a 'I'm not getting out of bed for that salary' way. If it is about the salary, then try something like this:

'I know that I can make an impact on the advertising department targets and was hoping for a salary in the range of £££ to £££,' or

'I'd like a salary in the range of ££££ – is this something we can discuss?'

It's probably a good idea to give a reason first – how good you will be; then your proposal – how much you want. It's not always about money, though. It could be about training, holiday entitlement or hours of work:

'I really want to work for you, but my current employer is offering me the chance to do a marketing course – is that something that you might be able to offer?' or

'You say the hours of work are 9am till 1pm – I'm wondering would it be possible to start at 9.30am and finish at 1.30pm so that I fit in with the train times?'

And finally if they put you on the spot and ask what salary or terms you want, be prepared to spell it out. Research the market for the work you do and find out what the reasonable pay level would be. If you are considering graduate positions, the website Prospects gives a good guide to what salary to expect from a range of graduate jobs – see www.prospects.ac.uk.

If there is a demand for your skills, and there is a shortage of applicants, you are in a stronger position. Here's a possible way to answer the 'What salary do you want?' question:

'Depending on the whole package, I would be interested in a salary in the range of ££££ to ££££.'

The figure you actually want is the mid-point of the range you give them.

What if you don't want the job and are offered it?

If, having been interviewed for a job, you decide it is just not for you, it is better to phone up immediately and withdraw yourself from the selection process. You could say something like:

'On reflection, I have realised that this job isn't for me, and I would prefer not to waste your time any further. Thank you for interviewing me.'

What if you are really not sure whether to accept a job offer?

Buy yourself some time by asking for 24 hours to think about their offer, then weigh up the good and less good aspects of the job, matching yourself against the job realistically. Talk to a careers adviser/personal adviser or someone you trust and then make your decision.

Turning a rejection into a future job offer

Asking for feedback after an unsuccessful job interview is the way to improving your skills and building your confidence back up. Most good organisations offer feedback or a debriefing after an interview, so ask them about this. Frequently, this debriefing means that you have an informal conversation with this employer. Use it to find out if there are other jobs that may suit you. This is how one feedback conversation went:

Kelly	Thank you for agreeing to give me some feedback on my interview performance. Can you give me any pointers for improvement?
Recruiter	We were all impressed with how you interviewed – you came across as capable and well prepared. The person we appointed had just one skill that you didn't have – she had a qualification in deaf sign language – and we thought that would be extremely useful as many of our patients in the surgery are deaf or hard of hearing. Other than that, you were equal to our selected applicant – that just gave her the edge.
Kelly	I'd still love to work for you – if I started deaf signing classes, would that help me if I apply in the future?
Recruiter	We have a holiday period coming up in a few months, if you took deaf signing classes and came back to us in July we might be able to start you on a temporary contract.
Kelly	Thank you – that's good advice – I'll do that.

The long wait for the offer

It can seem interminable waiting to hear about an interview decision, and it's difficult to gauge when to wait and when to take action. As a general rule, you should ask the question at interview – 'When am I likely to hear about the result of this interview?' and then if you haven't heard in their timescale, you can phone up. Otherwise, something like a five-day gap ought to be long enough, and any time after that you could phone and ask for their decision. The only exception to this might be with large recruitment interview situations when an organisation is interviewing a large number of people over a few weeks – in that instance you might allow a two-week gap. Remember though, that making that follow-up phone call suggests confidence and keenness, so do it in a proactive, positive way.

You should be getting to the stage now where the whole interview process seems to be becoming more familiar and manageable, so let's move onto the last few aspects of interviews that you need to know so that can feel an expert.

10

And just one last thing …

Most interviews follow a fairly predictable format, as discussed so far, but it's worth considering what might be called the 'unusual' interview situations that just might come your way. As a general rule, the higher the stakes or the more competitive or unusual the career, the more challenging the interview might be.

For example, there is a relatively recent career called Abseiling Window Cleaner or Rope Access Worker (for more information, see *You Want to Do What?!* Vol II, published by Trotman), and it's likely, as part of the interview, you would be expected to show off some abseiling skills. Similarly, for those exciting jobs in media, TV or advertising some rather different interview formats might be used. First, let's take a look at the use of presentations as part of an interview format.

Being present as a presenter

When you are offered an interview, the invitation to interview might ask you to be ready to deliver a 5–15 minute presentation on a particular topic, which you will be questioned on afterwards. All the previous advice on preparing yourself for interview still applies, including using your personal resource state and practising cognitive rehearsal (see Chapter 6).

Added to this, you need to recognise the presentation as another way that they will be assessing you. It may be that as part of the job you will need to do presentations to customers, so they want to know how you will come across. There are whole books devoted to the art of giving presentations so I am just focusing on some key points and tricks that you can be aware of.

Prepare your topic and decide on three or four key points you can make reasonably in the time.

Plan an interesting introduction that gives an idea of what you plan to cover and offers a little surprise – perhaps offer a short anecdote or funny story to do with the topic – this can help relax you and the interviewers. Here is an example:

Jenny

Jenny had been asked to give a presentation to a travel company on the topic of 'Interesting travel destinations'. She began by saying the following:

'We often hear the saying "It's better to travel hopefully than to arrive" and in my gap-year travels, it was often the case that just getting to my destination proved more interesting and challenging than my arriving at my actual destination point. Nothing quite went to plan, but nonetheless it often transpired that arriving somewhere unexpected (as a result of changes in travel arrangements) proved more exciting than all my wildest imaginings of where I had thought I might end up.

'Now I want to focus on some of those interesting and unexpected travel destinations and show how if I worked for Travel Travel I might be able to tempt your customers to book exciting holidays.'

What Jenny did was to use a personal anecdote to lead into the topic. She also brought in her passport to use at the end to show the exciting frontier or customs stamps she had from different countries and how each one brought back memories. Doing this makes the presentation real – Jenny is fully present and because she is talking about something personal and fun this makes her relax.

Move around when you talk because again this is more natural and your voice will project better.

Know the points you want to make backwards and forwards so you barely need to check your notes.

Powerpoint or overhead slides can help, but if you can talk through your presentation without these prompts, then you are well prepared and you should barely need them. Use them if it helps your audience. Make sure that whatever you do use is clear and have only two or three points on each slide. It's good to use a question as a heading to invite your audience to think or to encourage their involvement. Jenny, for example, had one slide with the question 'Do you know where you're going?' and another one which read 'Telling them where to go!', which is an amusing way of catching attention.

Finish with a flourish and signal you are coming to end with a phrase like 'And so what I want to leave you with …' or 'And in conclusion …'. If there is a quotation from a famous person or even a cartoon character you can use, then that can make for an upbeat ending.

Overall, try and show enthusiasm for your topic, take some good deep breaths before you start, see yourself doing it brilliantly and then just do it – no one much likes giving presentations, but they can be managed with some courage and preparation.

Be present! What this means is that you are focusing on the moment and not allowing yourself to be distracted by negative thoughts and irrational fears. In his way you will be fully available to perform and answer questions interviewers might ask. If you're really smart, you may find you have answered all their potential questions in your presentation!

Other unusual interview parts

For marketing, media and advertising careers, there is a chance of some kind of real-world trial connected to the job role. For example, some trainee journalists were given three hours to find the telephone numbers of three or four famous celebrities who were ex-directory. Can you think how you would do this?

The successful applicants used their contacts, the Internet and libraries to find the agents of these celebrities, explained that this was just an interview game and succeeded in getting some contact numbers.

A TV company gave applicants a messy in-tray from someone's desk (an in-tray is where someone puts the work they mean to do) and gave the scenario that this person had gone off sick and the candidates had to decide what should have priority and what should not. They then had to justify their decisions. They were given one hour to make the decisions and write their short presentation.

These kinds of interview game rely on your ability to think fast, make decisions, or consider more than one point of view – it would be impossible to practise or prepare for them, except by expecting the unexpected. If this happens to you, stay calm and focused and then take decisive action.

The 'Columbo technique'

Beware the 'one last thing' question. This is how it works. Just like the wily TV detective, an interviewer might save a tricky question until last. Just as you think it's all over, they launch their favourite and most challenging question. Don't be fooled into taking this last one lightly – it may be the clincher, so just watch out!

A confident interviewee might try to do the same back to the interviewer. It may be that, just as you are about to leave, you ask,

'Oh, by the way, what do you think makes your company a good place to work?'

This might seem a cheeky question, but it may be appropriate for an 'in your face' kind of radio station – they might view it as proactive and confident.

It's not a good idea to ...

You might think that you would never be so cheeky as to ask an assertive question like that last one, but there are plenty of other things that you ought to avoid doing at interviews. The following are just a few based on feedback from people I know:

- DON'T smoke in the car before an interview – even if you need to smoke. Smoking in an enclosed space means that your hair and clothes smell of smoke as you walk into the interview.
- DON'T have a quick alcoholic drink on the way for the same reasons.
- DON'T talk about how you hate your present employer.
- DON'T use phrases like 'Even though I don't know much about ...' – it's your job to tell them what you *can* do, not what you *can't*.
- DON'T cough or sneeze over people.
- DON'T forget to check yourself in a mirror before going into the interview – do a nose check (blow it clear!), a teeth check (food stuck between teeth), button check (all buttoned up), clothes check, anything-else check (turn all the way round in front of mirror).
- DON'T have a large bag to carry – it makes it difficult to shake hands with people.

My last 'don't' would be 'DON'T BE SCARED!' I know that's easy to say, but I would suggest that you think of yourself as courageous and a little excited instead. Every time you rise to a challenge like an interview you act courageously, and you notch up one more bit of confidence – 'I can do that!' So think of yourself amassing confidence like a treasure through the process of a series of brave acts. And if all else fails, try acting 'as if' you are confident – do it enough times and you really will be acting naturally!

WINNING
CVs for first-time job hunters

2ND EDITION

KATHLEEN HOUSTON

'For a busy student adviser seeking a handy reference book to help first-time job hunters, this publication should provide all the information needed.' Courses-Careers.com on the first edition

Getting that first job is an all-important step in every person's life but how do you go about it? One of the first things you'll need is a CV. But you need to know exactly what that is and what should or shouldn't go into it.

This book answers all of the major questions you need to know before you can write and submit your first CV. Covering work experience, gap year, part-time work and full-time jobs it includes:

- Examples of ideal CVs
- Advice on covering letters
- Information on tailoring the CV for the type of job you want.

August 2004
0 85660 971 4
£9.99

Order online at www.careers-portal.co.uk and save 20%!

WINNING
job-hunting strategies for first-time job hunters

GARY WOODWARD

Winning Job-Hunting Strategies is about giving you confidence in job hunting and equipping you with an array of skills and techniques to help you land the job you want. It is aimed primarily at those who are new to the job market, or those who may be returning to work after a significant break.

Taking you through the whole job-hunting process as well as effective strategies, it includes information on:

• Generating career ideas
• Researching your options
• Sources of vacancies
• Making winning applications.

July 2004
0 85660 973 0
£9.99

Order online at www.careers-portal.co.uk and save 20%!